PATTERNS OF
FAMILY PLACEMENT
Current issues in fostering & adoption

Joan D Cooper

ERRATUM

Due to a printing error, the last sentence of paragraph 5 on page 44 is incorrect, and should read as follows:

Localisation rather than parochialism is the objective and, in support of this, there is firm commitment to the London Boroughs 'Mums and Dads Campaign' (page 91) and to co-operation with neighbouring agencies so that fostering at a distance only becomes imperative when there is no alternative.

National Children's Bureau

Patterns of Family Placement
Current issues in fostering and adoption

Published by
National Children's Bureau
8, Wakley Street, London EC1V 7QE
(*Telephone: 01-278 9441*)

First published September 1978
© NCB 1978
SBN 90281 715 9

Printed in Great Britain by
Avon Litho Limited
Masons Road
Stratford-upon-Avon
Warwickshire

Design: G A Clark

775476
6000887765

Contents

Acknowledgements

The development of this issues paper was sponsored by the Lothian and Strathclyde Regional Council's Social Work Departments and the Scottish Office Social Work Services Group — a commission that was greatly welcomed by the Bureau. This report results from their initiative and from the co-operation of those statutory and voluntary agencies which generously and genuinely shared their recent experiences in developing family placement for children. My thanks are due to all of them and especially to those who spent effort and time describing their policies and in supplying first hand accounts of experiments. In addition, the staff of the National Children's Bureau, in particular Peter Wedge, Gillian Pugh and David Fruin have offered suggestions and comments and Kathy Hedgley has borne the brunt of the secretarial work. I have also had invaluable practical help from a friend, Muriel Fleming, and stimulus from Nancy Drucker, Nancy Hazel, Alexina McWhinnie, Ruth Nothmann, Christine Reeves and Jane Rowe. The errors and misconceptions are mine.

JOAN COOPER
July 1978

Introduction

The scene described and the issues raised in this report are those of the Autumn of 1977. The scene is ephemeral. Some of the issues, by contrast, are more permanent because they relate to individual rights, sometimes conflicting ones, to corporate and to personal responsibility and to the distribution of power. The issues concern not only rights and obligations and the reflection of current public attitudes but, when applied to individuals, relate to emotional attachments and strong feelings which defy logic and procedural niceties. This enquiry has disclosed that current fostering and adoption practice is in a state of transition. Conventional attitudes and cautious policies are being challenged and people are asking whether family placement should be considered as an option for all children who, for long or short periods, cannot live with their own families. But always in the background is the question of whether many of these children could live in their own homes if the appropriate resources were available. Yet resources are only appropriate when they are relevant to specific needs, available at the right time and in the right place. This state of adequacy has never been reached in the past and is unlikely to be attained or even attainable in the future. Hence, one of the main issues is about the compromises and the tensions which underlie efforts to capture the elusive 'best' when it is only the 'good' or the least damaging that is a practical possibility.

In 1977, the Strathclyde and Lothian Regional Council Social Work Departments, together with the Scottish Office Social Work Services Group, commissioned the National Children's Bureau (NCB) to produce a report within a period of about six-months concerning recent trends and issues in fostering and adoption sevices for children in the care of statutory and voluntary agencies. Their intention was to use the report in developing their policies in relation to children in care and their families. It was agreed from the start that, after presentation to the sponsors, the report should be made generally available by the National Children's Bureau.

A professional liaison group, comprising representatives of the three sponsoring bodies, of the University of Edinburgh and of the Scottish Group of the Association of British Adoption and Fostering Agencies (ABAFA), was appointed to offer advice and guidance as the project developed. This group met three times during the period of the preparation of the report and was singularly unparochial in sharpening-up some of the issues.

The basic information contained in the report was obtained from responses to a written inquiry sent by the NCB to all regional council social work departments in Scotland, local authority social services departments in England and Wales and voluntary adoption and fostering agencies then in membership of ABAFA. Information from Northern Ireland is not included as adoption policy and legislation there is under review. Eleven out of the 12 Scottish departments, 88 out of 109 English departments and four out of eight Welsh departments responded. Twenty-five out of 56 voluntary agencies replied. The non-confidential material supplied by respondents is available in the NCB library for reference purposes. In a few instances there was discussion with and visits to statutory and voluntary service giving agencies. The project descriptions which are included have been authorised by the agencies concerned. Information was also generously given by ABAFA, the Adoption Resource Exchange (ARE), the National Foster Care Association (NFCA) and by individual practitioners and researchers.

This report does no more than give a brief account of the efforts made to open up opportunities for children and families who have missed-out in the past as well as for those who need opportunities now and in the future. It concentrates solely on recent and proposed developments in fostering and adoption but such concentration is in no way intended to underestimate preventive and rehabilitative services. Further, besides being ephemeral, the report is inevitably impressionistic and unsystematic. Responses were received over a four-month period from September to the end of December, 1977, so that the information related to no exact point in time; indeed some respondents deliberately delayed their replies until agreement had been reached over the introduction of a particular policy or project. However, the purpose of this report is to review current issues rather than to present a statistical picture; the emphasis given is necessarily subjective and limited by the work that could be undertaken by one person in just over six months within a limited budget. The projects which are briefly described have been chosen to illustrate different models and attitudes. On the whole, the projects figured among the earlier responses. Some equally interesting schemes, received later, have had to be omitted. Nevertheless, the thinking, the planning and the activity reported suggests that the scene described, however ephemeral, is a dynamic one. Above all, a deep human concern was rooted in the search for effective and satisfying family placements.

Chapter 1
Family placement

Most children have been nurtured and prepared for family life in groups based on tribal arrangements or a network of family relationships within which the task of child rearing was a shared responsibility. In the United Kingdom during this century the size of families and the size of households have both shrunk dramatically so that the nuclear family of two parents and two children living in the jealously protected privacy of a small house has come to be regarded as the normal family pattern. In this situation any kind of child exchange, or host and guest relationship, is particularly sensitive and delicate.

Although fostering, and more recently legal adoption, have been well recognised ways of securing family life for children unable to live with their natural parents, they have never been the normal child rearing pattern. Both fostering and, more particularly, adoption have been circumscribed by law in an attempt to arrive at some kind of balance between the harm done to children by lack of family experience and the risk of unnecessary filial deprivation of natural parents. Law and regulation represent society's wish to see some notion of 'fairness', to respect the social system of marriage and child rearing and to support the task of every generation in the rearing of its successor generation. Nevertheless, the law remains a blunt instrument for managing intimate and sometimes passionate human relationships. This inquiry has shown that the limitations and strengths of the legal framework for fostering and adoption were well recognised by the respondents. They were sensitive to diverse and sometimes conflicting human aspirations which lay behind so many fostering and adoptive situations. 'Excellence' in practice was only excellence when family placement was the most appropriate and creative response in particular circumstances and was not an end in itself. Respondents stressed that the first question to be asked was when and in what circumstances was placement away from the natural family necessary and justifiable?

Replies to this inquiry suggested that family placement was seen as but one option among a series of alternatives which included domiciliary, day and residential care, together with the mobilization of any or all of these resources to enable children to live in their own homes. But when they could not do so and family placement was an appropriate resource, fresh initiatives and developments were beginning to change the image and ex-

pand the possibilities of fostering and adoption. These changes were occurring unevenly and were creating both enthusiasm and resistance.
Nonetheless, it emerged that there is an unmistakable trend towards regarding fostering and adoption, with variations in time-span and legal status, as
two elements of one-family placement programme and not as distinct and
separated activities.

Setting the scene: fostering

Fostering does not automatically command the kind of universal approval
given to those who nurse the sick or educate the young. It has not yet
achieved the middle class 'seal of approval' reserved for adopters. It starts
with doubts and questions about who ought to be doing what for whose
child and for what kind of reward. A major issue about fostering is that of
its esteem and prestige.

All societies have had to make arrangements, normally through the family into which a child is born, for his transformation from the helpless
dependency of infancy to the relative autonomy of adulthood. This
transformation, or process of socialisation and humanisation, takes about
a quarter of an average lifetime and creates emotional and social ties of
reciprocity that can themselves last a lifetime. These emotional ties, formed
from close relationships, so often misnamed 'blood-ties' when they occur
within the biological family, cannot be measured in a test tube. But neither
can prejudice be so measured, though it remains a powerful influence in attaching labels, sometimes favourable, but mostly unfavourable, to all concerned with the placement of a child in a new family where new emotional
ties may or may not be formed. Given this unpredictability, fostering is
unlikely ever to be free from public or private tensions.

The ideal, for the individual child, is to be raised in his own loving,
healthy and competent family devoted to securing for its children satisfac-
tion and status in all the desirable spheres of life. To have to seek anything
approaching the ideal in another family too easily becomes a reproach to
the family of origin, a reproach to the child because special arrangements
call for special effort on his behalf, and also a reproach to the alternative
family whose motivation may not be understood and who may be relieving
parents of their obligations or denying them certain fulfilments.

Fostering is not only open to moral questioning but also to a sentimental
curiosity about those who open up their families to someone else's child.
What sort of emotional and financial reward is due to them and what kind
of social approval can they expect? The legacy of the Poor Law scarcely
allows fostering to compete with those occupations which society has so far
respected and rewarded accordingly. This is not surprising, since memories
of the Poor Law include putting out young children to wet-nursing and ap-
prenticing older, now called adolescent, children to trades likely to equip
them to become economically self-supporting adults in the long run but using them for cheap labour in the short run. It is not difficult to see why

fostering has for so long had a low financial reward, a low profile and low public esteem. Many of the issues surrounding it relate to its history and image.

Setting the scene: adoption

Adoption generally speaking has enjoyed high public esteem. It has a relatively recent history in the United Kingdom as a formal and legal process, being first legalised in England and Wales in 1926 and in Scotland in 1930. There has been a recent decline since a peak was reached in 1968. In that year almost 25,000 adoption orders were made in England and Wales. Nearly one-fifth of these were, however, adoptions of illegitimate children by parents and not adoption by strangers which is the more commonly understood meaning of adoption. In Scotland, too the number of adoption orders has fallen during the last decade (*Table 1*).

In earlier centuries and in other cultures, adoption was concerned with religious observance and with the inheritance of a family name and property. In this country and in this century adoption has been generally assumed to mean the transfer of rights and responsibility for a child up to his age of majority from the natural parents to other adults. Adoption has inherited elements of altruism, charity and convenience, with legal safeguards against the exploitation of any of the parties concerned.

Adoption has a legacy of esteem in that voluntary organizations, usually of religious and charitable origins, have played a larger part than statutory bodies in adoption placement. Its heritage is philanthropic. It was only in 1958 that legislation clarified beyond doubt that local authorities had the power to act as adoption agencies and thus gave recognition to adoption as a secular as well as a religious activity.

Adoption has had other characteristics which differentiated it from fostering. Until fairly recently it has been much concerned with finding babies 'fit for adoption' for childless couples. It has been an area of social work largely practised by women and concerned with early mothering and peripheral fathering rather than with parenting. It has also been, characteristically, a secret process in order to preserve the anonymity of the natural parents and to recognise the child's total integration into a new family when adoption was by strangers. It has been a separatist and specialised area of practice significantly influenced by law and constrained by judicial process.

One of the aims of the most recent piece of legislation, the Children Act, 1975, was to promote the provision, by regional and by local authorities, of a comprehensive adoption service through their own activities and in conjunction with approved voluntary adoption agencies. The intention was that an historically inherited patchwork of adoption services should be replaced by a universally available service, publicly provided, and forming part of a comprehensive range of personal social services for children.

National economic restraint has delayed the full implementation of the Children Act, 1975. It may well prove that social and demographic change is now becoming as influential as the legal framework in shaping the future of adoption as a social arrangement for parents and children. The birth rate has fallen during the last decade. It may be, though this is speculative, that reliable contraceptive methods and an increase in abortions has actually reduced the number of unwanted children. Less stigma and improved, if still difficult, economic and employment opportunities for single mothers have made it easier for them to keep their children. In England and Wales, since 1967, the number of illegitimate births and the number of illegitimate children adopted by non parents has fallen (*Table 2*).

The traditional demand from childless couples for physically healthy white babies with a relatively favourable hereditary background continues but the number of such babies who are free for adoption has sharply declined. There is no immediate prospect of a reversal of this pattern and, for the future, the impact of assisted insemination remains an unknown factor.

The current scene

Traditional fostering and adoption patterns have changed during the seventies. In the past, both have suffered from cautiousness, lack of research and resources. Fostering has finally to overpower the legacy of the Poor Law if it is to become a positive programme for the care and treatment of a wide variety of children ranging in age from birth to eighteen years. Adoption has either to continue to decline or to extend to older children and children with special needs. This kind of adoption may well require financial provision and acceptance of the child's links with the past.

Fostering still suffers from confusion and ambiguity about its role and purpose. There has been comparative clarity about short stay, often emergency, fostering used in a family crisis. The foster parent had a clear, occupational role, and the task concerned the warm and comforting care, usually of a young child during brief separation from the parental home, and the goal of return to that home was not in doubt. Short stay fostering in preparation for an adoption placement or, more rarely, for assessment prior to permanent placement (ABAFA, 1977) had a clear purpose. In contrast, the uncertainty of intermediate and long stay fostering with their lack of definition of task has constantly been shown to promote insecurity for all the parties. Moreover, this uncertainty has produced children who spent many years in care with tenuous parental contact so that restoration remained a possibility rather than a probability (ABAFA 1977).

The distinction has been drawn between 'inclusive' and 'exclusive' fostering. The former acknowledges the child's background as his own heritage and accepts his parents, his social worker and the role of the placement agency. Fostering described as 'exclusive' absorbs the child into the foster family (Holman, 1975). This distinction has helped to pinpoint, and perhaps to explain, the ambiguity, confusion and disillusionment with fostering from the middle-sixties onwards.

Many of the new initiatives described in this report may well be a response to recognition by foster parents and by social workers that it has become necessary to bring greater clarity to the task and purpose of fostering. If this were achieved, there could be a radical change in its image. Fostering is developing more diverse patterns but also more specific goals and tasks which reflect the work which needs to be done with a particular child and his family. Foster parents are sharing responsibility with the placing agency and are informing themselves and the public about the nature of fostering.

In contrast, the current scene in adoption is affected by uncertainty as to its potentiality for a group of children varying widely in age and condition. This uncertainty has placed many of the smaller voluntary agencies in a dilemma about their future. Some have been able to extend the scope of their work to provide social work for families; some have negotiated to provide adoption services either for or in partnership with statutory bodies; some have closed down and some regard their future as problematical.

Adoption and fostering are but two ways of meeting the needs of children (Pringle, 1974) and are becoming aspects of a family placement policy which is developing momentum. This policy is modifying the attitude of agencies, the role of the social worker and the function of residential establishments. These changes are not occurring without the critical appraisal of the public, the media, the professionals and, importantly, of the children and families concerned.

Chapter 2
Indicators of change

It would be easy to account for stagnation in fostering and decline in adoption as due to the combined effects of the reorganization of the personal social services, the consequent dissipation of skills and changing social attitudes towards marriage and child rearing. It is, however, important to look at some other factors which have also influenced patterns in family placement. Among these are:
1. demographic trends;
2. research and literature: fostering;
3. research and literature: adoption;
4. 'Children Who Wait';
5. American and European influences;
6. consumer participation.

1. Demographic trends
A characteristic of children now in public care is that fewer of them were young children under five when received into care. The proportion of young children has dropped in relation to other age groups when compared with the composition of populations of children in care in 1966 and 1956. Agencies which intend to pursue a vigorous family placement policy for children now have either to face up to developing the placement of older children or to abandoning the policy. An examination of statistics over a twenty year span, undertaken by Prof. Roy Parker as chairman of the NCB working party on substitute care, is reproduced here with his permission *(Table 3)*. An interpretation of the statistics inescapably leads to the conclusions that a family placement policy must be concerned essentially with children over the age of five, particularly boys, with young people over school leaving age and with children who have appeared before a court since this is now the legal status of over half the children available for family placement. Fostering within a kinship network has become a decreasing option so that a family placement policy means the active recruitment of new families. It is the current patterns of children in care that define the target population from which appropriate homes can be found.

It is interesting to speculate on the reasons for such a rapid and comparatively recent change in the structure of the population of children in care *(Tables 3 and 5)*. In England and Wales, the Children and Young Persons Act, 1969, has been held responsible for an increase in the number of older children in care but Scotland had no similar legislation. Although the figures are difficult to interpret meaningfully because of changes in the measuring system and in the definitions used, the number of children in care in Scotland appears to have increased and the percentage of children in foster care to have dropped. The raising of the school leaving age has also been held to be a contributory factor. At the lower age range, the falling birth rate itself and the reduction of the number of hospital admissions for mothers in childbirth could have affected the number of young children needing to be received into care. The situation could have been achieved by a variety of factors such as the increased provision for women and children subjected to marital violence, the extension, however limited, of playgroup and day care facilities together with the more active part played by fathers in the parenting of young children and the increased and more diversified use of home help services. Such speculation is less fruitful than recognition of the implications of current demographic trends which gives urgency to the needs of older children and to the problem of children staying in care for long periods and growing to adult status with little or no experience of family as distinct from institutional life.

Demographic change and interest in different categories of children has seen the introduction of two new terms into child care rhetoric: the 'hard-to-place' and the 'special need' child. The first of these labels is attached to children who do not immediately fit the expressed aspirations of traditional foster parents who avowedly hope for 'exclusive' fostering and expect to receive young children. Fostering for babies and young children has for so long been seen as the first priority. Older children may be hard-to-place because of their consciousness of their own roots, biographies and identities and their consequent resistance to speedy and total integration into a different family with its own life style. Older children are more likely to have siblings. They are able to play an active part in working towards reunion with their own families when this is a realistic possibility. Older children may have more complex behaviour patterns and may have developed educational difficulties. It has always been thought that boys are harder to place than girls during latency and puberty though the sex preference of foster parents may turn out to be different for adolescents. 'Hard-to-place' tends to be used as an imprecise category which may well include those who are thought by themselves, by foster parents or by social workers to have characteristics which make the search for appropriate family placement more extensive and more subtle.

The second category, the 'special need' children, are those suffering from mental, physical or emotional handicaps or behaviour problems to such a severe degree that any family-life experience must include treatment, in addition to care, and positive acceptance of a programme designed to meet the special needs of the particular child. The meeting of those needs will cause considerable disturbance to the placement family's normal life style.

Both categories converge in some individual cases and both have given rise to new developments in fostering and adoption.

The categories are not new, though the numbers within them may be greater or attitudinal changes may have caused more children from either category to be seen as requiring a family placement. Hence, it is fair to ask whether the labelling represents a genuine recognition of an extension of family placement for children who would not have been considered for such a placement in the past or whether the labelling is used to attract the degree of support and quality of service that is, in fact, required for all forms of family placement. The question is whether what is required is a shift from a philanthropic to a skilled activity that is recognised and rewarded as such.

It is also fair to ask how far family placement is seen as one of several treatment options, how it can be assessed as the treatment-of-choice in a particular case and how its success can be evaluated. This process of assessment and evaluation is essential if exploitation of children and families is to be avoided.

The thrust in family placement policy which is characteristic of the last few years is not only related to the recognition of the changing structure of the population of children in care but is, additionally, a response to the legacy of children who were identified (Rowe and Lambert, 1973) in the early seventies as forming a hard core group likely to spend many years in residential care unless a more positive family placement programme could be developed for them. Research and literature have also questioned assumptions about fostering and adoption.

2. Research and literature: fostering

The 1970's started with a questioning of some of the popular and professional assumptions about fostering. Victor George's study of fostering (George, 1970) and studies by Kraus (Kraus, 1971) and Napier (Napier, 1972) confirmed poor success rates in terms of unexpected breakdowns. Studies have tended to find success rates of forty to fifty per cent. But a fifty-fifty chance could be used to argue for or against a social policy based on fostering. Such a situation provides fertile ground for ideological loyalty rather than scientific support for extending fostering. Poor success rates, a lack of hard theory for decision making and consequent difficulties in developing standardized fostering practice could not enhance the image of fostering or increase the confidence of practitioners. In spite of poor success rates, fostering during the seventies has, nevertheless, been developed and diversified.

Other studies have drawn attention, not for the first time, to the confusion over the traditional role, without any clearly defined legal status, of foster parents acting as substitute parents or as co-workers or therapists.

(Adamson, 1973 and Holman, 1975). Concern about fostering policy and practice together with public and media interest led to the setting up by the Government of a professional working party charged with the task of producing guidelines to good practice (HMSO, 1976).

The most recent review of the research and literature relating to fostering (Prosser, 1978) has concluded that the position is still that little is known about the long term effects of placement and that there remains a lack of recent studies comparing the adult adjustment of children who have experienced different types of care.

A descriptive analysis of the fostering scene in the seventies (ABAFA, 1977) drew attention to the confusion over various kinds of fostering, the ambivalence over parental contact and the contribution of fostering as one of a series of options for children whose own parents could not care for them or could only care on a partial basis.

In general, the research and literature produced in Britain during the seventies has presented a depressing picture.

At this point there are two matters which merit consideration:

1. available research and literature tend to have been concerned with the placement of young children so that there is a need for immediate investment in study and research relating to the current experiments in fostering older and complex children;

2. in the longer term, a restricted knowledge base may, if continued, far out-weigh the temporary consequences of recent organizational upheaval, dilution of services and dissipation of professional skills.

It is not only in Britain that questions are being asked about the effectiveness of fostering policies. Two recently published American studies disclosed a situation regarding length of stay which is not dissimilar from the picture here. Both studies identify work with parents as a critical factor in relation to the rate of discharge from care. New York City data were collected for a longitudinal study, which covered a five year time span, of 624 children aged from birth to twelve years who, for the first time in their lives, entered foster care during 1966 and remained in care for a minimum of ninety days. Allowing for the cultural and administrative differences and for the heavy concentration, in this sample, of black and Puerto Rican children drawn mainly from single parent households, the findings still have some significance for this country.

The first of these studies (Shapiro, 1976) found that the goal of family rehabilitation, though a basic social work tenet, was not consistently realised. While it was clear that concentration of skills and resources during the first two years in foster care, a term that is more widely interpreted in America, contributed significantly to the discharge rate, rehabilitation gradually became less important as a goal and contact with natural parents decreased as time went on.

The second study of the same data (Fanshel and Shinn, 1978) found that 36 per cent of the sample of children were still in care at the end of five years but that over half of this particular group were at that stage unvisited by their parents; essentially, for all practical purposes, they were experiencing parental abandonment. This research raises, in a dramatic form, the question of whether 'drift' in long term foster care ever really offers stability and fulfillment to children, foster or natural parents.

Another area of research has been concerned with the fostering of complex children. There is as yet little available research in this country but Kalveston's study of 40 Swedish foster families is of interest (Kalveston, 1973). This study concerned families prepared to work with hard-to-place children. As families, they were distinguishable from the Swedish population as a whole in that the foster families lived in the country or in small communities. They tended to be self employed people; generally wives were working at home and, without being rich, the families were good budget managers. They had a wide age range and most of them had children of their own who were either grown up or teenagers. Kalveston sums up the findings:

If our findings are pointing in the right direction it would then be right to look for foster parents for difficult children among people whom we have generally seen to be satisfied with themselves and their conditions and at the same time are armed with some type of surplus — of human interest, energy, mental capacity, intelligence, and last but not least, time. All these being resources of which they do not make full use until they get a difficult foster child. Such a surplus can most often be found with people who think that they have succeeded well in bringing up their own children. It is, however, important to state that the same surplus is available in families with small children and with people without children.

3. Research and literature: adoption

The 1970's started with a query about the survival of traditional methods in adoption. 'The survival of practice, and whether it continues to be in the hands of social workers, may be dependent on how far the latter are prepared to look critically at their work, to view new concepts with an open mind and be ready to try innovations and use findings from research studies' (Triseliotis, 1970).

American and other research into the effects of adoption on older children – (Bohman, (1970) Jaffe & Fanshel, (1970) and Kadushin, (1970) – has suggested a not unfavourable outcome. In this country, the longitudinal study of adopted children, aged seven, who formed part of the National Child Development Study (Seglow *et al* 1972) confirmed the findings of most earlier researchers that quality of family life in the adoptive home was more significant for a satisfactory outcome than a child's heredity. The most recent study (Tizard, 1977) concerned a sample of 65 children who, as infants, entered residential nurseries for long term care. It was found that, within this group, those who were subsequently adopted were more fortunate than those who were restored to their natural families and indeed, the restored children did rather less well than a comparable group of London working class children brought up in their own homes. On IQ tests and reading attainments, the restored children showed a lower performance than the other groups and also had a higher proportion of nervous symptoms and behaviour difficulties. All their mothers had been indecisive or reluctant about reclaiming them and, in more than half the restorations, there was little close attachment between mother and child.

The restored children either returned to a single parent or to the home of a step parent who often showed an open preference for his own younger children. By contrast, the adoptive mothers had a strong desire for a child, were prepared to devote endless time and patience to him and were willing to tolerate immature and often difficult behaviour. The adoptive fathers also seemed deeply committed to the adopted child.

Most of the natural families in the study had too many problems in their lives and too few resources to be able to spare the time and thought needed by children returning home from institutional care. The most successful restorations were to single mothers who had few other commitments. Unlike the adoptive parents who had struggled to get a child, the natural parents had left their child in an institution for between three and seven years, visiting him, if at all, irregularly and infrequently. The study concludes that it is difficult to justify the practice of allowing parents to leave children in care for years if further research confirms that, when the children are restored, they may not receive the love and demanding care that they require.

A further study which has been influential during the seventies is Rutter's reassessment of the ill effects of maternal deprivation during early childhood (Rutter, 1972). While accepting that the bond of affection between the mother or mother-substitute and the child may often be stronger than other bonds, Rutter posited that separation need not always involve bond disruption and that other bonds might be or become significant in a child's life experience. Love and harmonious family relationships during middle childhood were found to be important to conduct and to behaviour.

It is the dearth of research, the lack of validation of findings, the small size of many of the samples and the nature of the sample chosen which, taken together, have failed to provide a reliable base for practice but have, nevertheless, succeeded in raising important issues. The four key questions that continue to trouble anxious policy makers and practitioners alike are:

In what kind of circumstances and for what category of children is either long term fostering or adoption the treatment-of-choice?

If it is established that family placement is appropriate as the preferred form of treatment, then is adoption so much more emotionally secure than fostering that a move towards adoption is justified?

Is a shift of resources required in order to ensure that there is a heavy investment in restoration, immediately after parental separation and during the first year, so that early restoration, in reality, becomes a basic goal for the majority of children, however and whenever placed?

If restoration is found to be impracticable or even damaging, is it then important to make a decision and plan for permanence in placement?

4. 'Children who wait' *extended the importance of looking and raised questions about it*

A study published in 1973 covered 2,812 children then being cared for by 33 British statutory and voluntary agencies. It was highly influential in questioning attitudes and practice (Rowe and Lambert, 1973). The children were aged under 11 years and had been in care for at least six months. The study found that in the opinion of social workers, 25 per cent of the children studied (or a national estimate of over 6,000) needed permanent family placement. The children were mainly over the age of two years. (For further evidence of the age structure of children in care, see *Table 3*). Many had already been in care for a large part of their lives and a high proportion of them were boys or were members of sibling groups or were children from minority ethnic groups, — mostly full or part West Indian.The study prompted some agencies to look at the population of the children in their care and to examine the situation in their own geographic area. It seems that the agencies which took action responded in four main ways to the dramatic findings of *Children Who Wait:*

1. detailed surveys were undertaken, chiefly in 1974 and 1975, by at least a dozen statutory authorities;

2. another dozen or so authorities preferred to categorize and quantify selected groups of children who were thought to need family placement. These authorities concentrated on more limited targets within the population of children in care, such as all children of nursery age, all children under ten, single children of any age, sibling groups, or boys but not girls over the age of nine years;

3. one group of authorities participated in surveys carried out by a consortium of agencies in a demonstration exercise mounted by ABAFA and the University of Leicester in 1977. This study, which is to be published shortly, showed that five authorities in one region estimated that 280 children under 14 years of age needed long term foster homes and a further 70 children needed fostering that might lead to adoption;

4. some authorities accepted the evidence of *Children Who Wait* and modified their statutory reviews of children and assessment procedures to build in family placement as an option to be considered for every child in long-term care.

More precise knowledge about the composition of children in care raised a number of questions:

Should resources be geared to family placement for the easier to place children as a first priority?

Should a home-finding exercise for a selected target population of young children be preferred because, if not placed soon, these children might grow up without real family life experience?

Should older children who had already missed out have a special programme of their own?

Should family placements be classified on a length of time (short or long term) or nature of task (care or treatment) basis or on a combination of both?

Should family placement be seen as an adequate policy to meet the needs of an area which produces a high ratio of children needing alternative care or, in such a situation, should family placement be one component of a wider intervention strategy?

5. American and European influences

Theory and practice have been influenced by American literature and teaching. The influence of ABAFA has been crucial in this country in making available the North American professional attitudes, knowledge and skills that might be appropriate to statutory and voluntary agencies here. For more than 250 agencies and members, ABAFA provides professional advice, conferences, literature, teaching material, training kits and publicity. American experience of homefinding for hard-to-place and special need children has considerably influenced positive publicity for the community education and recruitment of families and the practice of group work in the selection, matching and training approaches to family placement.

ABAFA, in conjunction with the Central Council for Education and Training in Social Work, broke new ground in this country in introducing 'Spaulding For Children' as a prototype agency for the adoption of hard-to-place children. The papers given at a course addressed by Kay Donley, Spaulding's Director, were subsequently published under the title *Opening New Doors* (ABAFA, 1975). 'Spaulding for Children' was founded in Michigan in 1968 in the family farmhouse of Warren Spaulding and has since specialized in placing for adoption children with multiple handicaps within an age range from infancy to 16 years. In the United Kingdom, 'Spaulding for Children' has influenced two experiments described in this report: Parents for Children in London and Barnardo's New Families Project in Glasgow.

In fostering, the concept of defining targets, tasks and time limited goals for all those involved in a placement has been markedly influenced by the concept of task centred casework (Reid and Epstein, 1972). Within a system of time limited treatment for specified goals set out in an agreed contract, their approach has been applied for treatment goals in social work with children, with natural and with alternative families.

Some European countries have emphasised family placement, rather than residential care, as their preferred policy on the grounds of therapeutic benefit rather than financial saving. Sweden, in pursuing fostering for all ages, has developed four principles. These are:

1. normalisation or family rather than institutional treatment;
2. localisation or the maintenance of local geographic and community ties;
3. agreement to placement goals; and
4. participation or shared decision making to allow for the creative involvement of all those concerned in a placement.

An account, as brief as this one, of influences derived from the experience of practice in other cultures raises several questions:

Is the situation and the need in other countries comparable to the position here, and if so, is there evidence that policy and practice responses adopted there are effective?

Is it appropriate to import policies and practice from other countries without careful tests of their viability in this country?

Is research and practice sufficiently well founded to form a basis for developing family placement as a social policy?

Is it known actuarially that family placement is a cheaper policy or is this a specious form of arguing for a policy based on an ideology?

Is indigenous practice so insular that there is resistance to innovation?

Is there hard evidence to suggest that preventive work designed to support children in their own homes is achieving desired results?

Is it necessary for preventive work and family placement to be in conflict?

6. Consumer participation

Both fostering and adoption, as aspects of family placement, have attracted rising citizen and media concern during the last decade. Brief accounts of three voluntary associations, formed to extend the concept of family placement, illustrate this concern. They are Parent to Parent Information on Adoption Services (PPIAS), the National Foster Care Association (NFCA) and the Voice of the Child in Care.

The voices of some children who experienced care have been heard through the Bureau's project and publication 'Who Cares?' (Page & Clark, 1977).

Parent to Parent Information on Adoption Services

In 1971 a group of parents interested in the adoption of children with special needs formed an information service (PPIAS) to help families to find children who needed adoptive homes. Their concern has been, and is, with permanent family placement for black or racially mixed infants, for children, irrespective of age, who have a physical or mental handicap, and for older children.

PPIAS has now more than 50 local groups working to collect information about potentially adoptable children, other than healthy white babies, and to provide practical help and support for families who adopt special need children. They operate under the slogan 'Every child has the right to a home and somewhere there is a home for every child'. Their newsletters, issued three times a year, give first hand, personal and intimate accounts of experiences in adoptive families and pen sketches and photographs of children awaiting adoptive homes. They also distribute news and views about developments in fostering and adoption. Whilst permanent foster homes are sought for children who are not free for adoption, the main goal is adoption but without necessarily completely severing ties with all members of the first family.

National Foster Care Association

Since its inauguration in 1974, when a number of isolated local groups of foster parents formed a national body, the association has become an umbrella organisation for over 140 groups and 36 corporate members. As a national pressure group, it aims to improve foster care services. It seeks to represent the views, aspirations and grievances of foster parents and others involved in foster care both to central and local government, to the media and to the public. It is financed by a government grant, by membership subscriptions and by fund raising activities.

While elements of unionisation are not absent, NFCA essentially seeks to raise the image of fostering, and to provide local and national forums where all concerned with foster care can share experience and mobilize opinion. It is also concerned to press for specific training for social workers and to involve other professionals, for example, health visitors, in foster care. It encourages local groups, gives precise guidance to them on constitutional procedure, supplies information and canvasses group opinion. As well as furthering an educative, democratic and grass roots involvement in major issues, NFCA makes demands for the recognition, training and fair treatment of the occupational group which it represents. To this end, it analyses the nature, scope and value of that occupation, issues a quarterly newspaper for foster parents and maintains international links especially with its American counterpart.

Currently, the issues which have been identified by and are of concern to NFCA include:

1. *The unity of foster care.* The principle that fostering is an indivisible and

all-embracing activity which has varying goals, tasks and relationships with other social services.

2. *The use of professional and salaried fostering schemes.* These are seen as devices to create a privileged elite for a selection of labelled children who, in reality, represent all children in care, but who, for historical and demographic reasons, have, until the last decade, been denied family placement as a method of care and treatment.

3. *The need for research.* More information is needed about the reasons why, out of about one hundred thousand children in care, only some forty per cent are in family placement.

4. *The position of natural parents.* The concept of filial deprivation is accepted. The need to work with the natural parents intensively, particularly during the first year of separation, is recognised in order to achieve restoration if this is a practicable and creative aim.

5. *The revision of the* 'Boarding-out of Children Regulations' (*England and Wales, 1955, and Scotland, 1959*). As NFCA perceives the regulations, they are designed to secure that the child is, at least temporarily, the property of the agency. They are regarded as authoritarian in tone: the conduct of the placing agencies is spelled out with the intention of protecting the child and scheduled supervision is elevated to a recipe for safeguarding the child even though he is entrusted to family care for 24 hours a day. In contrast, the association sees the need to replace this approach by ensuring that the foster parents have a defined participative role, access to medical and social information and involvement in planning and decision making. NFCA wishes to replace the outmoded and confusing 'undertaking' which foster parents are required to sign. Instead, it seeks a contractual arrangement which, in line with modern fostering, shares the responsibility between foster parents and agency, assigns tasks to each and mobilises resources. NFCA does not question the need for regulations, but regards the categories of those who may become foster parents as unnecessarily restricted, and anticipates more broadly based guidance which pays due regard to the appropriate roles of the agency, the foster parents, the natural parents and the child.

6. *Publicity for fostering.* The presentation of a realistic image of modern fostering to the public by means of regular and unremitting publicity through the media, through local groups and by means of the distribution of literature and aggressive rather than diffident propaganda is thought essential.

7. *Allowances.* NFCA recommends realistic allowances to foster parents based on rates deriving from the National Family Expenditure Survey as an alternative to professional or salaried schemes. NFCA proposes enhanced rates to cover extra services rather than payments tied to the alleged difficulty of the child. It sees these enhanced rates as reaching up to four times the basic rates and paid as a supplement. The supplement would cover such extra and essential items as laundry, domestic and relief help, telephone,

heating, accommodation, travel and other extras incurred in sharing a particular lifestyle. Such allowance would, it is hoped, be free.

8. *The preparation and training of foster parents and of social workers.* A report on this has recently been published (NFCA, 1977).

9. *Relationship with social workers.* NFCA is pressing for foster parents to be recognised as colleagues sharing a skilled child care task with social workers. It is also pressing for an appeals procedure to provide an avenue for foster parents' complaints.

In short, NFCA sees itself as concerned to enhance the public image of fostering and the self-esteem of foster parents and of foster children.

The Voice of the Child in Care

The Voice of the Child in Care began in 1975 as a multi-disciplinary network of people concerned with the interests of children growing up in care. It aims to make known the facts about children in care and to explore ways of raising standards of professional practice. Without resorting to national publicity, membership has grown to over a hundred individuals, living predominantly in the London area, but having links with individuals living elsewhere. Regular quarterly day conferences for the total membership are held in North London. Several developments are occurring:

1. a pilot scheme for 'Children's Spokesmen' at statutory reviews of children in care has involved a group of lay volunteers in a six months' training programme based in London;

2. a co-operative exercise is being undertaken with the Personal Social Services Council for England and Wales to study complaints and appeals procedures for children in care by collecting examples of children's rights being either protected or abused;

3. a group of young people who have grown up in public care has been formed and this group will be offered residential weekends and quarterly conferences where they can express their views and feelings;

4. a working group of members who meet monthly is exploring such issues as professional standards, reviews of children, specialisation in practice and the question of inspection.

The Voice of The Child in Care gives expression to the view that at present children in care have no true rights and no voice. Care Orders or the assumption of parental rights give the agency and its staff almost complete power and direction over the lives of children who have little protection against poor service, bad practice or arbitrary decision-making. The Voice of The Child in Care is a pressure group to represent the needs of children in care and to help them represent themselves. It is concerned with, but not restricted to, their need for family placement.

'Who Cares?'

In 1977 a statement by a group of children in care on how they perceived and experienced their lives was published. The first step towards this publication was a conference at the National Children's Bureau attended by 100 children aged 12 to 16 years from 28 local authorities in England and Wales and from two voluntary agencies. Following this conference some 16 children and 8 adults (four of whom had themselves grown up in care) formed a working group and produced this document which illustrates how care is perceived by the children, how it stigmatises them and sets them apart; and how difficult it is for them to share their concerns even with caring and responsible adults. The children discussed the particular difficulties awaiting them on reaching their 18th birthday and many other problems which arise from being in care. The group also drew up a *Charter of rights for young people in care* and a challenging list of the things they wanted to change. This list is reproduced here:

1. Give us a chance to find a voice and to speak and mix with ordinary people so that public attitudes about care can be changed for the better. Set up 'Who Cares?' groups throughout the country.

2. Give all young people in care a chance to attend their own six monthly review. Give us a say in who attends, besides the social worker, his boss and the people we live with. Young children need someone to speak for them. Learn how to talk with us and learn how to listen. Give all children in care a voice in their life.

3. Do away with the order book and special voucher system for buying our clothing. It will save money if we are allowed to shop in ordinary stores — not just the most expensive ones. Do away with special tokens for paying for our school dinners.

4. Help residential workers and field social workers to find ways of working more closely together than they do at present. They should stop pulling in opposite directions, against the children.

5. Bring pocket money and clothing allowance into line nationally so that most children of the same age get roughly the same allowance. Children should know how much the allowance is and what it is expected to cover.

6. Help us to have a realistic approach to sex education and personal relationships. Enable us to learn how to look after ourselves — not suddenly at 18 expect us to know all the things we've never had a chance to learn.

7. Help us sort out our education while we're young. A lot of us have missed out on our schooling through being in care and moving from place to place.

8. Make sure every young person in care really understands his situation and why he cannot live with his family. Give us factual information — a booklet or leaflet — to explain care and the laws that affect us. When we leave care, make sure we know what help we can reasonably ask for and expect to get.

9. Ask local authorities to decide whether or not corporal punishment is allowed in their children's homes. Children in care should know what the ruling is and who they can turn to for help if they think they are being ill-treated. This is delicate but it can be done.

10. Find ways of letting us help children younger than ourselves. Give us something to work for while we are in care!

Chapter 3
Recent initiatives in fostering and adoption

The pressures have been mounting during this decade to develop family placement. These pressures have derived not only from public, economic, theoretical and professional interests but also from the impact of small demonstration projects as yet not all well grounded in theory and tested by results. Brief descriptions of a number of schemes are given to illustrate the current variety and impetus towards experiment.

Special schemes

The first set of descriptions of projects illustrates schemes for finding families for those who are loosely defined as hard-to-place and special need children. The labels represent categorizations made by placement agencies and run the risk of being self fulfilling. For the future, the degree of difficulty in placing and sustaining children in satisfying placement may well be determined by the experience of some of these and other similar experiments, provided that rigorous measures of evaluation are applied to them and the results made public so that comparisons can be made and principles can be further applied and tested.

Berkshire and Reading schemes

The first three salaried foster parents were employed in Reading as early as 1971. There is now an establishment in the Reading division of Berkshire for 14 families appointed on a regular salaried basis and ten have been recruited since 1975. The annual salary of £2,326 is payable whether or not a child is currently placed. This salary includes the fostering allowance for the first child. The appropriate fostering allowance is paid for a second and any subsequent children concurrently placed and there is a variety of extra allowances available. Part of the salary is deemed payable as renumeration for the use of the 'professional' foster parents' home as their place of work and the salary attracts superannuation.

Recruitment is through advertisement. Only the wife of the married couple is appointed on a salaried basis but the husband is a foster father and placements are with the wife and husband jointly. Applications are also considered from single women and widows. The women are expected to have either qualifications or experience in child care. There is a rigorous selection procedure. This includes informal and formal interviews, and assessment of the applicant's background, experience, ability to manage stress, the capacity of the applicant's family to tolerate the intrusion of a disturbed child and discussion with referees.

The children placed are teenagers and others who may have behaviour problems and children of any age with special needs which arise from mental, physical or emotional handicaps. They are children who require individual care and a planned treatment programme which can best be provided in a family setting. The concept of fostering is extended to include treatment in the sense of defining and working towards the achievement of goals.

'Professional' foster parents are not regarded as surrogate parents, but encourage the children to keep in touch with their natural parents who have complete access, the hope being that the children will eventually return to their own homes. These foster parents are called upon to undertake what is more of a domiciliary social work task rather than that of a traditional parenting and caring role. The placement of children follows a carefully designed procedure except in emergencies.

Training is through a series of regular seminars, and, as professional members of the department's staff, these foster parents referred to as foster 'care workers' are invited to attend area team meetings. They also formed a mutual support group meeting monthly on an informal basis in their own homes.

The expectation that older rather than younger women would be more likely to cope with the demanding tasks required of them has not been proven. More recently appointed foster care workers with a professional background and with their own very young children have been able to offer the time, energy and expertise to older children placed in their care on a short term basis. On the other hand, some foster care workers appointed earlier chiefly for long-stay children, who have had a child or children placed with them over a period of years, have experienced considerable stress, and it has become apparent that they need some form of periodic break. This can be arranged for the more recent appointments who have undertaken to work on a short term basis with a difficult adolescent. These foster parents can be allowed a break of a few days or longer between placements. A few families have withdrawn from the service because of the stress caused by the unrelenting demands made upon them. It has been found to be essential that some arrangement should be made for breaks in the domiciliary care and treatment of long-stay children.

A specialist principal social worker in Reading has managerial and supervisory responsibility for the scheme and regularly visits the placement families. Responsibility for the children remains with the appropriate social workers. The latest position is that 19 'professional' foster care workers have been appointed since 1971 and during this period five couples have resigned and been replaced. Out of a total of 71 children placed, five have been removed on account of difficult behaviour. These professional foster care workers are appointed for different tasks; four take children selected for long term placements, five take adolescents for assessment or short term treatments, five take adolescents for long term placements and one home takes children of any age group. There may be up to 22 children in placement at any one time.

Berkshire, while maintaining the salaried scheme, has now recruited three fee-for-service freelance families receiving a discretionary allowance of £24.50 per week. These families participate in a selection process, receive training and regular support through fortnightly meetings with salaried families and through the help of a specialist social worker.

The National Children's Home
The preparation of this scheme started in September 1975; the first placements were made early in 1976 and had reached eight by the Autumn of 1977. The distinctive feature of the project lies in the emphasis it places upon rigorous selection and the formal, theoretical training of foster parents willing to care for complex children. This project embraces both long and short stay homes but it emphasises long stay placement for children who have usually already experienced at least two years' residential care. The children include those with mental or physical handicaps, emotional disturbance, speech difficulties, backwardness (retarded development whether physical, mental or social), behaviour problems and those who are not always easily integrated into a family or locality because of age, colour or breakdowns in previous fosterings.

The additional weekly payment of £29 (index linked) in addition to fostering allowances is regarded as a 'contract allowance' to compensate for the wife's lack of earnings from outside employment rather than as a salary. The payment is symbolic of the expectation that families are providing skilled care and treatment rather than substitute family life or parental relationships. Selection is based on the 'hurdle principle' of accepting applicants who respond to local publicity and survive a lengthy procedure. This includes answering a rigorous questionnaire, attending one or more group meetings involving professional staff including a consultant psychiatrist. The group is followed by systematic semi-structured home interviewing of individual family members and of the family as a whole. There is then a more informal home interview by an independent social worker (a member of the NCH staff who is uninvolved in the project) whose task is to evaluate the couples on a five point scale of expectation of success. Selection for the next stage, which is a course of training, is then undertaken by a panel using a points system. Commitment to twelve training sessions is then required and afterwards there is an appearance before a final selection panel to determine eligibility. The decision to appoint couples as participants in the scheme is finally made and signifies the start of payments and initiates informal group meetings for further training which is aimed at creating and maintaining agency loyalty, providing support, furthering learning experiences and providing continuous practice-based feedback for the NCH.

From the moment of actual placement, the foster parents become colleagues of agency staff and have access to information, records, meetings and to educational opportunities. In their work-role, these foster parents are perceived of as comparable with residential staff and there are expectations of skilled performance in the work which takes place within a family.

In this scheme the agency relies on a process of professional selection rather than on self or mutual selection for participation in the project. Its main features are that it is intended for long term placements of children of all ages who present out-of-the-ordinary demands, that it pays what amounts to a salary for skilled work based on vocational training, builds in agency loyalty and is so designed as to make monitoring, evaluation and research important and integral aspects of the project.

Mid-Glamorgan Special Foster Parent Scheme

The scheme is designed for the placement in foster homes of children who need family placement but who would not be acceptable in the usual range of foster homes and who would otherwise stay in residential care. The children are those with physical or mental handicaps; and children, including adolescents, with behaviour difficulties and families of three or more siblings. This is Mid-Glamorgan's second scheme. In replacing an earlier one, this scheme included higher rates of payment, training, and a more specific categorization of children suited to placement. It started in 1977 and so far 28 children have been placed with 15 special foster parents.

Children considered for the scheme are carefully assessed, preferably using a multi-disciplinary approach, in either a residential or community-based setting. It is considered to be particularly important that the special needs of each child are clearly identified and that, in total, their needs add up to a firm recommendation for family placement.

Foster parents included in the scheme are those who have experience, training and/or skills beyond those normally expected among traditional foster parents. Special foster parents may be people with experience in their own professional or personal lives which fits them for caring for children with difficulties. Thus, the procedure for accepting 'normal' foster parents may well be modified by introducing specific training for the fostering task.

Special foster parents receive a flat rate fee-for-service of £30 per week for the task of caring for children selected for the scheme in addition to the normal fostering allowances. There can be a discretionary payment for the cost of domestic help for up to 15 hours a week where this is needed and particularly in the case of handicapped children or when several children are being cared for in one family; refunds can be made for the cost of a sitter-in subject to prior departmental approval. In some long-term cases, especially where difficult or handicapped children are being cared for, it is recognised that the foster parents and their own family members may need a break. The residential and foster care resources of the department may be made available to provide the break.

If, in the course of time, a child's difficulties (e.g. behaviour problems) are resolved, the special flat rate allowance is continued. The grounds are that his problems might recur and also that the family budget would be upset if payment were withdrawn and the foster mother might then have to seek employment outside the home. The allowance is designed to attract people who prefer to have a job looking after children in their own homes.

Haringey Long-term Care Group

The long-term group was originally set up in one area in Haringey in 1973. It is now placed centrally and carried responsibility for two hundred children in 1977. It comprises a team of seven social workers (several part-time) with administrative and clerical support and is led by a principal social worker. Children are transferred to the long-term care group from the area teams if their social workers leave and when the children have no home or parent living within the boundaries of an area team. Many of the children have either no links or very fragile links with their natural parents. In most cases there is either a court order or the authority has parental rights.

Because the group concentrates on these potentially isolated children, it is possible to give them a more intensive and efficient service. The aim is to provide, through a team of social workers who agree to work for at least three years in the department, an opportunity for each child to build up relationships which will give him some sense of security and of personal worth. Whenever possible, the plan is to place the child in a permanent home even if some children have to be placed at a considerable distance. For those older children for whom family placement is not possible, the group aims to make sure that the child has the best experience of life which is available in the circumstances. The hope is to have a 'responsible caring adult' identified for each child in order to secure that there is at least one person who is significant in his life and who is not constantly changing. Sometimes, however, the only 'parenting' which is available is through the sustained social work support and involvement of the group itself. Children who are identified as being particularly at risk of being or becoming 'isolated' in the sense that they have no place in a permanent family are included on group camping and youth hostelling expeditions so that they can build up relationships with several members of the long-term care group. There is close liaison with residential social workers who, for some children, are identified as the 'key worker'.

If a child has to move home, the group regards the event as similar in its effect on the child as a major surgical operation. 'Intensive care' is then provided, if necessary by a team composed of, for example, the social worker, the educational psychologist, a home tutor and the people actually caring for the child. In this situation, there is a residential resource (a foster home run by the principal social worker) available for emergency and short-term placements. This foster home also provides a holiday place for several older boys who are at boarding school and a 'home base' for other older children. The ability to help and to have resources available in a crisis is regarded by the group as vital in attempting to build up a sense of trust and confidence in the child at a time when he most needs support.

During the year ending September 1977, area teams in Haringey passed 17 children to the long-term care group. In September, 1977 the group was responsible for 76 children in foster care, 52 children in residential homes, 15 in boarding schools, 15 living in their own homes and a further 15 living in lodgings, flats or other kinds of accommodation which included bed and breakfast provision. By the end of 1977, 13 of this large group of children had reached the age of 18, three had been legally adopted, five had returned to their own homes and the care orders had been revoked or parental rights had been rescinded for seven children.

During the period January to August 1978, a further 20 of this group of children will reach the age of 18 and 11 children are expected to be legally adopted. By June 1978, the forecast is that the total number of children for whom the group will continue to be responsible will be about 145. This will give an average case load of 30 children for each social worker and it is hoped that this ratio will enable the group to achieve its objectives and provide the children with the security and opportunities that they need until they reach adulthood. Theoretically, as the backlog is reduced, the number of long-stay children needing this intensive support should be reduced.

The long-term care group works on the principle that in agencies where there is a number of children growing up in care, there is a need for a specialist group to work alongside traditional adoption and fostering officers. Many children who might have been regarded as too old or too difficult for placement have been found adoptive or foster homes because the children were well known to the group which could identify the psychologically right time for placement to be attempted. In other circumstances, and without this intimate knowledge of the child, the placement opportunity might have been lost.

Strathclyde Quarrier's Family Project
Quarrier's Family Project is a joint experiment between Quarrier's, a large voluntary home for children, and the Strathclyde Regional Council's social work department which is responsible for the majority of placements in Quarrier's. The aim is to find adoptive and long-term foster homes for 41 of the 500 children. Nineteen boys and 22 girls, mostly of school age, who have little or no contact with their parents have been identified as suitable for fostering. An advertising campaign launched the scheme in the Spring of 1977 and so far 27 children have been placed. One of the hopes is to find substitute parents for families of two or three siblings.

A special regional team of four has been set up to work closely with the staff of Quarrier's and with Strathclyde area teams. The project is being monitored by a member of the Strathclyde regional research unit.

Barnardo's New Families Project

The Barnardo's New Families Project based in Glasgow is a three year demonstration exercise which hopes to illustrate the potential of non-traditional forms of adoption. Its purpose is to find permanent new families for children growing up in care who have no realistic chance of a return to the natural family. In some cases freedom for adoption is recognised as not beyond question. So some of the children are not only within the category of hard-to-place but they also may be subject to judicial decisions which reject adoption. This is one of the associated risks until case law is established.

This project is founded on the belief that there exist several groups of families who are willing and competent to parent hard-to-place children. Firstly, there are families of parents and children who share humanitarian motivation and skills in creating a dynamic family life which is sufficiently relaxed and open to be able to incorporate an additional child, or more than one. Secondly, there are married couples who have come to terms with their own childlessness and who already have relevant training or experience with children. Thirdly, there are quite 'ordinary' couples or individuals, who may or may not be childless and who with training, education and regular support can make a success of the adoption of complex school-age or handicapped children.

The project has been set up initially for three years but its life will be extended if it proves its value to the regional authorities referring children. It is restricted in the number of placements by the ratio of approximately one social worker for six children. Emphasis is put on preparation of these children for placement as well as on locating the right families. During the first year, the project received 194 inquiries from people who were considering adoption and about 20 per cent of these inquiries became firm applications. Between November, 1976, and December, 1977, 16 children have been placed and one of these has been legally adopted.

The objective of this scheme is to attempt to prove that small, intensive projects can succeed in finding and supporting adoptive homes for hard-to-place and special need children. The hypothesis is that to do so is highly cost-effective as well as providing a better quality of life for the children concerned.

The project is intended to provide a model which could be incorporated in a statutory comprehensive adoption service.

Parents for Children: London

Parents for Children is a voluntary agency which was set up in 1976. It resulted from three main factors: the pressure of adoptive parents, chiefly through PPIAS (page 25) to get children out of institutions and into families which it is insisted can be found for most children; the increasing evidence from ARE that there were more and more children being referred for adoption who would never be placed unless a special effort were made on their behalf; and the inspiration of visitors from the USA who were involved with specialist agencies for children with special needs and were successfully finding homes for these children.

The need for a specialist agency became increasingly apparent. If ARE was to retain its function as a co-ordinating agency it could not without confusion become a demonstration project for child placement. Parents for Children was to concentrate on home-finding for the hardest to place children who would otherwise experience institutional rather than family care. The age range extends from 0 to 18 years and the younger children tend to have severe emotional and behavioural problems. Parents for Children aims to specialise in the recruitment of families, to develop the skills needed to locate them and then to support them in a parenting task. A placement might start with fostering but always with adoption in view and always with the offer of continuing service for as long as necessary. Parents for Children has placed eight children during its first year and undertaken introductory work with eight other children.

Parents for Children is backed by a time limited grant from government and from trusts. In addition to its home finding activity, it has educational, study and publicity functions. These are aimed at testing out the belief that even the most demanding children can have the experience of family life and that there are families willing to offer this opportunity. Parents for Children operates within a radius of a hundred miles from London for the recruitment of families. It accepts children from the London Boroughs and from the Home Counties. Already it faces the problem that this geographical limitation means that families from outside this area might well be better suited to an individual child than the families available in the South East.The question of whether a highly specialised agency should be national or regional remains unanswered. But Parents for Children, like Barnardo's New Families Project, offers a model for replication either in statutory or voluntary organisations.

In the seeking of family placements, Parents for Children makes active and unremitting use of the press and the news media and is recording the number of homes recruited according to the type of publicity used. Publicity about individual children is realistic, even blatant, in describing positive attributes but in no way disguising disabilities, usually several of them, or the demands likely to be made. Some children help to describe themselves for poster publicity, and are able to stand face-to-face with their own descriptions and photographs and see themselves advertised as an illustration of the kind of child needing a home rather than as an individual appeal. A referral to Parents for Children involves acceptance of this type of publicity which tells the public no more than the child already knows about himself and his situation but actively involves the child in the process so that he knows that the publicity is part of a continuing attempt to find him a family. So far 21 local authorities have agreed to participate and to pay the fee-for-service of £1,300. This was based on the current equivalent of the average cost of a six months placement in residential care. For this fee, Parents for Children also undertakes to try to find a second family if, for any reason, a change from the family first chosen is needed.

Both the participating local authorities and Parents for Children have had to contend with the ambiguous legal status of many children. Links with parents or relatives may be virtually non-existent, tenuous or more positive but lacking any realistic possibility of the resumption of parental care. The children's legal status has remained indeterminate in that the local authorities have often not assumed parental rights. Parents for Children regard a resolution assuming parental rights as a prerequisite for a long-term family placement leading to adoption. An active search for families demands clarification of the status of the child whether he is living in hospital or in local authority care. This degree of security does not mean that agreement to adoption is necessarily given by parents at this stage. Parents for Children is finding many confused situations regarding parental interest and intention. They regard the meeting of the costs of disputed or technically difficult adoptions as an impediment which should be removed from families willing to offer an adoptive home for children who have severe disabilities and usually little or no experience of family life or positive and continuous family relationships. Parents for Children regard approved adoption allowances as essential for some of these children.

Referring agencies are involved in considerable work when Parents for Children accepts a child for intended family placement. A full profile of the child and the completion of the ABAFA standard referral form is a prerequisite. The child's social worker and the senior social worker have to attend meetings with the staff of Parents for Children so that there can be agreement on the division of work between the two agencies co-operating over the placement of the child. In addition, Parents for Children needs access to the child's file. Beyond this stage, it accepts responsibility for getting to know the child and for finding a family and working with both towards placement. The local authority buys a specialised service from a specialist agency to find and support a placement.

Parents for Children holds a monthly open meeting to which all inquirers are invited. The meetings alternate between Saturday afternoon and evening meetings. They may be attended by as few as three or as many as 30 couples or individuals who have responded to publicity. At these meetings, inquirers have face to face contact with adoptive parents, posters, case histories and social workers who know the children needing placement. Inquirers learn about adoption in general and the methods of work of Parents for Children. If they maintain interest, they are offered an individual interview followed by a series of educational group discussions. Only when they have had this chance of learning about this type of adoption are people asked to make any kind of commitment, to give any personal information or to fill in any forms. People interested in those children awaiting placement referral are given priority, others may wait until the kind of child they feel they could help is featured in the regular newsletter. Preparation for living with a specific child is the focus of the process rather than 'investigation' of them as parents in the abstract.

Parents for Children closely replicates Spaulding for Children (page 23). Its work is being monitored by the National Children's Bureau financed by a government grant.

Fostering projects for adolescents

Some projects for hard-to-place or special need children and especially schemes for adolescents have tended to be loosely labelled 'professional' schemes but this inquiry revealed no consensus about the meaning of this word (Pugh, 1977). When used, the term most frequently described schemes which involved a fee or a salary, required training for work to be done with a child and, in conjunction with the agency, with members of the natural family and sometimes with other people interested in becoming foster parents. It seemed to indicate interaction with the child and with others. It also seemed to signify colleagueship with agency staff. Generally, it was more frequently associated with the notion of skilled home-based employment than with the possession of formal qualifications for working with children. It has become a controversial term and may well have served its purpose in identifying special schemes and extending the fostering role.

Kent Family Placement Project

This project was established in 1975 to test whether it was practicable and effective within one social service department to develop a family placement policy for difficult adolescents (Hazel *et al*, 1976 and 1977). The scheme had certain hybrid characteristics in that some financial support was received from a charitable trust and the project was separately housed and staffed. The project was not established as an integral part of the bureaucratic structure; it was more comparable to a research and development operation within a large scale enterprise. The project is accountable to management but designed, within a life span of five years, to test out certain assumptions and processes which, according to the results of external and internal evaluation, will determine whether or not the scheme becomes permanent.

One of the particular features of the scheme is that, following a study made in 1972 by the Council of Europe's co-ordinated research group, the project derived much of its theory from European rather than from American policy and practice. Research has shown that among 17 European countries, some followed a pattern of family placement for all children, including delinquent adolescents, whereas other countries preferred a residential care pattern. The choice of pattern seemed to rest on history, tradition and ideology rather than on any scientific basis. The United Kingdom followed a compromise pattern by mixing foster and residential care as placement options. The Kent scheme also drew upon the work of Victor George (George, 1970) and his concept of foster care workers rather than foster parents.

The Kent project, drawing mainly on Swedish models, respects certain basic principles but it has now been in operation long enough to be generating theory from its own experience. These basic principles are:

1. normalisation or living normally in a family and as part of society rather than being segregated in an institution;

2. individualisation or the opportunity to experience a committed relationship with a few human beings who form a family and are willing to share their lives;

3. participation or equality of esteem and status to enable the four parties to the placement (the adolescent, the family of origin, the placement family and the social workers) to work towards voluntarily agreed decisions which affect their lives and work.

The essence of the Kent project is that families which have considerable emotional resilience and which practice open and frank communication are able to enjoy helping an adolescent who is experiencing difficulty. Given these conditions and motivation on the part of the family and the adolescent, it has been found that families in their own homes are able to carry out many of the tasks which have traditionally been assigned to social workers and teachers in an institutional setting.

In this project, which is a family based treatment programme for boys and girls aged fourteen to seventeen years, roles are clearly differentiated:

1. the foster parents are the primary workers acting as responsible adults and seeking help with their task when they need it. The task is that of helping the adolescent to learn about himself and to discover how his personality and behaviour affect and are affected by a small group organised as a family. The foster parents are not performing a substitute parenting role in relation to these near adults who are living with them;

2. the project-based social workers, in a colleagueship relationship with the foster parents, are recruiters, matchmakers, trouble-shooters and group workers since group work is the fundamental process for selection, matching, education and training and, much more recently, for policy analysis and development;

3. the social worker from the area team carries legal accountability for the adolescent in the care of the local authority. In consequence, he is also responsible for statutory visits to the foster home and for work with the natural family though this work may be shared with the foster family.

The Kent project, with its research emphasis, has defined certain principles which need to be tested in other settings. So far, the hypotheses are that:

1. positive and dramatic publicity, directed narrowly to the target popula-

tion of adolescents with severe social and behavioural problems, has produced few recruits from the traditional foster parent constituency;

2. the new parent constituency for this age group openly accepts financial motivation and reward for home based employment;

3. the shift in the balance of authority from the placing agency and social workers directly on to the family challenges some basic assumptions of traditional social work practice. These assumptions derive, in the main,from practice with much younger children;

4. good public relations to avoid destructive misunderstandings, as with all developmental work, is an issue not to be ignored. The forging and maintaining of public relationships, the time needed for testing out fact and fantasy, for research and monitoring is by no means a negligible factor in experimental projects.

Further hypotheses, which also require verification, arising from the experiment, include:

1. foster parents without formal relevant training but with learning opportunities can prove as successful with adolescents as foster parents with apparently relevant qualifications;

2. previous experience of parenting young children may be irrelevant to working with adolescents in a family context;

3. the adolescent's previous behaviour pattern is less relevant than his ability to think independently, participate in a contract and work in a setting and at a task which he has understood and consented to;

4. the contract is not immutable. Any of the parties may need to be released from it. Family circumstances, external change or a faulty contract may make transition to a different placement, with a new contract, the next positive step in the treatment plan for the adolescent;

5. boys tend to be more vulnerable than girls to seeking a 'criminal' solution to their conflicts, and working relationships with the police are vital;

6. contact between the adolescent, the foster parents and the natural family can vary from severance, through minimal and irregular contact to an increasingly close relationship. The feelings of natural families about an alternative family life for those adolescents of working age may or may not prove an obstacle as the placement proceeds but the reality of the relationships needs to form part of the contract from the beginning with allowance for development and change;

7. the contractual basis of the placement is a device for identifying and sharing rights, responsibilities and objectives in a clear enough form for all the parties concerned to understand and accept before they commit themselves to working out the contract.

The reports of the Kent project have identified certain processes which may, or may not, be appropriate to other projects. The normal local authority procedures are followed. Professional practice includes both home visiting and group work as vital elements. Home visits are used for initial clarification, discussion on specific issues and consultation with other family members. These tasks, vital in the early stages, may need to be repeated at any stage when circumstances change. Group work is used for support and learning and involves residential and field staff as well as foster parents. More recently, group work has been used to develop a more structured setting for consideration of behavioural and other problems. Easy access to psychiatric and psychological support has been found to be essential and there is a need for some form of crisis retreat.

In the three years to 1st December, 1977, 77 placements had been made and at that date 40 adolescents were in placement in 31 families. The current weekly fee is £37.31 paid in addition to the appropriate fostering rate.

Although the Kent project has acquired the image of a professional fostering prototype for adolescents, the scheme is now known simply as the Kent Family Placement Project. The word 'special' has been dropped from the title, perhaps as an act of faith to demonstrate that it should become normal practice to give adolescents in care an opportunity of experiencing family life outside their own homes.

Lothian Family Care Project

Lothian developed a scheme as a response to the great demand for residential accommodation for children aged 11–16. This was the age group presenting the most severe behaviour difficulties to residential staff and being cared for at a high cost of maintenance. In an experimental search for alternative resources for adolescents, Lothian social work department recruited initially five, now six, 'community carers' on a freelance, fee-paid basis to provide a place in their home for an adolescent in care. More funds have since been made available to the project.

Adolescents considered for placement are aged 11–16 years and are drawn from residential care. A child may remain in placement beyond 16 but it is intended that only one child should be placed with each community carer. The first programme, in March 1977, drew 55 inquiries of which 16 proved to be firm applications. After individual interviews and group meetings, five couples were accepted. No rigid criteria for selection for community carers have been adopted.

The community carer must be able to accept a particular adolescent for what he is and undertake a clearly defined task in conjunction with the department; for example, the task might be to provide an intensive one-to-one relationship with the adolescent or to follow particular treatment goals for a specified period. Support is given by a team of fieldwork and residential staff who select the adolescent. Community carers are expected to be willing to receive any training considered necessary and following a matching process to accept any child for whom placement is requested by the department.

The community carers are paid £1,500 p.a. for their work and the normal fostering allowance and certain additional out-of-pocket expenses are reimbursed. No retainer is paid during a period when no child is placed. The com-

munity carers are expected to give as much time to the child as his needs demand which means that they may not be able to hold other employment, but
the community carer's spouse may be employed. The scheme will be
evaluated by Lothian's own research and development section.

Strathclyde's Community Parents Project

The pilot Strathclyde Community Parents Scheme was launched in 1977 to
find homes for 15 difficult and delinquent boys and girls aged 11 to 15
years who were currently in four or five *List D* (formerly Approved)
schools, or awaiting *List D* placement, but assessed as needing family care.
Two children have been placed. The first year of the project is funded by
the Scottish Office and this funding may be extended beyond the initial
period. Community parents receive an allowance of £30 a week, tax free.

The main responsibility for the operation of the scheme rests with the
project worker. He is supported by an inter-disciplinary group which meets
monthly. This group is also concerned with research, criteria and procedures and for ensuring that the project attains its objectives.

The objectives are to select the appropriate children from the Strathclyde
area and to prepare and support the children before and after placement; to
establish a selection and educational programme for applicant families; to
create a pool of skilled foster parents and to prepare and support them in
their task.

All families who responded to advertisement by press, radio and television were invited, in small groups, to attend meetings in a *List D* school
where they could be given more details and speak to some children and
staff. Couples wishing to apply were assessed in accordance with
Strathclyde's guidelines and then attended a series of meetings for assessment and further information.

The community parents recruited were not necessarily 'professionals' in
the sense of having relevant professional training. The critical factors were
their motivation, emotional stability, ability to make relationships and to
work with children. A fostering assessment panel, including the project
worker, decided whether applicants should be accepted. This assessment
procedure ensured the integration of the project into the existing social
work structure.

Head teachers of all *List D* schools in Scotland were invited to select and
propose children as candidates for the pilot scheme. It was proposed that
the project be discussed with children and it was expected that some of
them would want to be considered. The project worker saw all the children
who were being considered but the selection was made by a panel consisting
of the project worker, the child's social worker and a member of staff from
the *List D* school.

The co-operation of other relevant services has been sought. Procedures
for the selection, placement and review of children have been discussed and
agreed with those concerned with the Scottish Hearing system.

Strathclyde's Education Department has agreed to provide advice and support in placing children in appropriate day schools. Because some children may be seen as difficult and disruptive by local day schools, individual tuition or day pupil facilities may be needed. The research section of the Scottish Office is responsible for monitoring and evaluating the scheme.

Wandsworth Adolescent Project

Wandsworth started a scheme in 1975 to place adolescents with local foster parents and made an evaluation in 1977. The scheme relied on a project worker operating separately from the fostering and adoption unit. The particular features of the scheme were specific advertising, preparation of the adolescent and the foster parents before placement followed by individual social work and group work support afterwards. Within a year eight adolescents had been placed. On a subjective social work assessment, in five instances, the adolescent and family were judged to have gained from the experience but three placements were regarded as unsatisfactory.

Inner London has always had the reputation of being a poor area for recruiting foster homes. For this project, the press, particularly the local Wandsworth quarterly newspaper delivered to every household, was found to be the best source of recruitment. The response to an inquiry was thought, with hindsight, to require an immediate social work visit rather than a letter. The families attracted to the scheme appeared to share certain common characteristics in that they enjoyed being involved with young people, wanted work and stimulus in their own homes, needed the extra income and had children under the age of eleven.

The adolescents concerned discussed the prospect of a fostering experience with a social worker five times on average before placement. They met the family twice before a trial stay. This process took about six weeks. Once the placement was made, the adolescent's social worker assumed responsibility from the project worker who, up to that point, had been responsible for all the arrangements.

Although pre- and post-placement group meetings were held in children's homes, groups were not an absolute requirement for the foster parents and the post placement groups were not held frequently enough to provide a regular source of support for them. Group meetings for interested adolescents were also held in children's homes before any placements were planned. The residential placement that the adolescent was leaving remained available for use in a crisis.

It was found that contact with the natural family was low and it was thought possible that the natural families felt at a disadvantage and needed more social work help. The processing of foster parent applications through a fostering panel was thought to be an obstacle to the project worker's task in that procedural delay could hamper the formation of relationships.

The main aim of the project was not to save money but to give adolescents an experience of family life and to discover whether families could be found within the inner city. A family placement represented a saving compared with a residential placement but the fee of £20 per week could not be regarded as particularly high for London.

This project was the first of two Wandsworth projects. In the course of the life of this first project, seven adolescents were placed one of whom was still in placement at the end of 1977. The project was evaluated by Wandsworth research staff which regarded the gains made as sufficient to merit further development.

Wandsworth is developing a second scheme but, this time, within its adoption and fostering unit. Unlike the first project, the new one aims at fostering children of all ages and adolescent fostering will be one objective of a more comprehensive scheme.

The proposed new project is time limited, based on a contract specifying treatment as distinct from the emphasis on care expected in a conventional fostering situation. Theoretically, it is the task rather than the child that is categorized after a close examination of the child's needs. Once identified, this task can be given time boundaries and can be made specific enough to be built into a contract. The planning stage, therefore, aims at an exact definition of the task; e.g., to achieve restoration to the natural home, to prepare for another type of placement or to carry out some specified form or method of treatment. In the planning and later stages, decisions by an individual worker are regarded as inappropriate and decisions are ratified by the adoption and fostering panel in a group situation.

The second Wandsworth scheme is intended to operate in an inner city area, to attempt saturation publicity and to test out the local urban capacity for the task of fostering. The principle of localisation is emphasised and is to be put to the test by concentrating home finding effort within the borough and adjacent areas before adopting a geographic dispersal policy. Localisation rather than parochialism is the objective and, in support of this, there is firm commitment to the London Boroughs 'Mums and Dads Campaign' (page 91) and to co-operation with neighbouring agencies so that house;

Family life experience for sibling groups

Sibling groups frequently figured among agency definitions of hard-to-place children and may seem more exactly to fit such a designation than some other categories. To provide a family life experience for several children of one family requires adequate accommodation which the modern three bedroomed house does not offer, full time commitment to home based employment, physical energy and emotional robustness. Agencies frequently expressed anxiety about the dual need to avoid separation of siblings while giving them experience of family life. One approach is described. On a strict interpretation of conventional fostering, Doncaster's scheme might be regarded as unoriginal but, nevertheless, it illustrates diversified patterns that are characterising modern family placement policies.

Doncaster Larger Foster Home Scheme for Families of Children

Two large foster homes were set up in 1975 with the object of keeping siblings together on a long term basis. The objective was solely to keep siblings united as a group but in the circumstances set out below:

1. when the siblings are a very closely knit group;
2. when one or more of the children may present behaviour problems if separated from the rest of the children in the family;
3. when it appears to be less demanding on the foster parents, even though there is more physical work involved, that siblings are kept together if the effort of maintaining close links at geographical distances is reduced;
4. when there are likely to be fewer long-term identity problems in adolescence if siblings have been brought up together so that they are less likely to feel alone, with no family to turn to as young adults, or to react by presenting problems which require specialist help.

Each foster home is used for the permanent placement of and the achievement of family life for seven children from two families. Thus four families have been kept together. The intention is that children will remain and grow up there until they marry or choose to leave home.

The scheme involved the social services department in purchasing and equipping two large houses which they let to two sets of foster parents at a fair rent but paid enhanced allowances to cover the costs of running the large house, providing for domestic help and for 'baby sitting'.

The foster parents were recruited from a short list of seven couples with considerable experience as 'normal' foster parents. Selection had to take into account the age of the foster parents for this long term venture, the size of their own family and the feelings of any existing foster children who had been placed with them.

The selected groups of siblings were carefully prepared and those with little or no parental contact had high priority. Where there was contact with natural parents or relations, plans concerning links were made.

The long term future has been considered. In due time three or four of the seven foster children in each home may have moved away and it has been recognised that the foster parents may then wish:

1. to move into their own house;
2. to move into a large council house with the remaining family;
3. to take another family of children.

The department and the foster parents have entered into formal contracts which cover such points as:

1. the tenancy of the house;
2. the department's agreed financial commitment;
3. the right to terminate the contract in the event of the foster parents proving unable to carry out the task;

4. the department's undertaking not to use the foster home as an emergency resource;

5. the foster parents' agreement that before any other person becomes long term or permanently resident in the home, the department's concurrence is required.

The foster homes are included in the responsibilities of the department's homefinding and adoptions section and a third foster home of this type is planned.

Short stay fostering for special-need children

Two schemes are described. They have been developed to provide emergency family placement for mentally handicapped children. Many agencies, in replying to this inquiry, were aware of the potential for relieving the stress and enriching the lives of parents of handicapped children, for giving institutionalised handicapped children a taste of family life and for working out such schemes with the National Health Service under joint financing arrangements.

Leeds 'Time-out' Scheme for Mentally Handicapped Children

This pilot project first operated during the summer of 1976 to provide family care, as distinct from hostel or hospital care, for mentally handicapped children whose parents needed a break or were facing a short-term domestic crisis. The contract was very specific in that the recruited families were to undertake to receive, one at a time, three young people who might be up to the age of 16 years, for up to 14 days each, during a 13 week period. There was a week's break between each placement.

The scheme involved cooperation with local voluntary organisations and the local hospital for mentally handicapped children. Press publicity announced the scheme which was sponsored by the Social Services Committee. An immediate social work interview followed inquiries. Six couples were finally recruited by a process of self-selection based on openly sharing with them the extreme difficulty of the task to be undertaken. The six couples involved in the project had, in all cases, some previous acquaintanceship with mental handicap. The training section and a local further education centre arranged a training programme for all the couples and two natural parents participated. The social work support system and the availability of an emergency hostel bed (not, in the event, required) were made explicit.

There was heavy social work investment in the preparatory stage. The transmission of detailed information about each individual child's unique behaviour, his specific needs and habits proved to be vital since it was found that a crisis in a placement nearly always related to lack of essential information. The commitment and resourcefulness of the families was beyond expectation.

This project had boundaries in that it was not designed as a residual scheme and did not have to accept all comers at all times. It was limited to what appeared to be, on a professional judgment, possible, practicable and in the best interests of all concerned in the particular transaction leading to a placement. The scheme was developed by social workers with a mental health background. It involved voluntary services for support and the health and education services for continuity of treatment and schooling. As a project, it was limited to a budget of £1,500 but it has now attracted joint financing with the Area Health Authority and is likely to be extended to an all-the-year-round programme for short-term family placements for mentally handicapped children. During 1977, 55 placements were made with 17 substitute families between 1st April and 30th October. From November, 1977, a phased or intermittent care programme has been developed, 32 placements having been made or planned. One of the interesting features of this scheme is that a similar project is also being developed to provide short stay care for elderly people.

The Somerset Pilot Project on Short Term Fostering for Mentally Handicapped Children in the South Sedgemoor Area

The main pressure for this scheme came from the parents of children attending a local day school for mentally handicapped children. Parents wanted temporary relief from the care of their children either at times of crisis or to enable them to spend a holiday or an evening or a day out with the rest of the family while still enabling the handicapped children to continue attending their own school. Initially, the parents demanded hostel facilities to meet their needs but their demands were resisted because local and national experience suggested that hostels providing short term care were economically unsound. Costs in such hostels are high and beds may be empty for weeks at a time. There was also a strong feeling on the part of social services staff that a more consistent pattern of care could be provided by a family setting in the community. The project was set up in 1976 and was reviewed with the parents in November, 1976, and continues to be regularly reviewed to ensure that it meets needs.

Initially two couples were appointed who got to know and understand all the children likely to participate in the scheme. These couples received training and support from the social services department. The couples are accessible by telephone to parents who are able to make direct arrangements for periods of short term care for anything from a few hours to a maximum of four weeks. Experience has shown that most families use the scheme for brief periods of up to 24 hours.

At the start, recruitment was primarily by way of the local press, radio and television. The local press article was most successful and several couples responded, but after visiting the special school and meeting some of the children concerned, some couples withdrew. Two were accepted; one had previously worked for the department as a 'special' foster parent and the other had had experience both as a home help and as a child minder.

Before these foster parents were selected and trained, all the families with a severely mentally handicapped child in the area were invited to take part in the scheme and 26 accepted; up to the present 20 families with children attending the day special school, including three pre-school children, and one child who is a weekly boarder at a hostel, have used it with varying degrees of regularity. Parents participated in the design of the questionnaire that was used to gather the necessary information about each child; this included many details of each child's daily needs and routine, together with a photograph.This information enabled the two couples to understand the child's daily routine at home, his interests and special difficulties. Perhaps because the parents were included in the design, they completed it with a wealth of useful detail. Initially each family was offered the use of one particular couple and parents and their child visited before any placement was made. As the scheme has developed both the foster homes have become available to all the families in order to provide more flexibility.

The admission procedure is simple: the parents telephone the couple and make arrangements for the care of their child either for that day or for a specific date in the future. Most of the children see their visit as more like a stay with a well known and well loved relative; naturally for those children who use the scheme less frequently, the relationship is less intimate. The parents contact the school to ask for the school transport to be diverted during a child's stay to pick him up from the short stay home in order to maintain his attendance at school. The parents have a 'cheque book' of care vouchers. This cheque book serves both to prove to parents that they have the right to use the scheme and to provide a simple administrative framework. In exchange for a period of care, the parents hand to the couple the appropriate number of signed cheques, and the couple returns these to the department at the end of each week. Payment can be made quickly and regularly on the scales agreed.

The maximum fee paid to the couples was fixed at £28 per week per child and the total cost of the scheme for a full year was assessed at £2,000. Similar schemes are now being developed in other parts of the county in close co-operation with four special schools. It is estimated that a further nine couples will have to be recruited and that the annual cost will be about £11,000 per annum, but this will cover an offer of service to about 300 families in the County. It may well be that the schemes in other parts of the county will not develop in exactly the same way. For example, it may not be possible to recruit enough couples who can provide such a full time commitment. One local society for mentally handicapped children has offered to assist financially for the first three years for a scheme in their area and joint financing money from the Area Health Authority has now been approved.

Emergency 'out-of-office hours' schemes

Many traditional short stay foster parents have willingly received children, usually infants, in emergencies and the inquiry revealed that this type of fostering remained a highly valued resource. Three examples of schemes devised to make use of emergency fostering as a resource out of office hours are described. They are not related to any particular category or age of children. One comment made was that, unless regularly used, emergency foster parents may find the work boring and unsatisfying. Another was that permanent out-of-office hours duty teams may well be effective in reducing the need for emergency reception into care.

Wakefield Emergency Scheme

A scheme to develop the use of about 12 foster homes for out-of-office hours emergency placements was started in 1976 as an alternative to admission to residential care. The scheme began with six homes and 24 children had been placed up to April, 1977. Where necessary, telephones were installed in the foster homes; rental, together with the addition of £1 per quarter to cover the cost of official calls, is paid. The usual fostering rates and allowances are payable and any extra expenses individual to the child placed are met. There is no retainer fee. Support and the management of the detailed administrative arrangements, together with the continuing assessment of the fostering resource has been made the responsibility of the local social worker. The scheme is regarded by Wakefield as practicable and successful. One of its characteristics is the importance attached to the assessment of the child and family situation during the first 10 days and to restricting the child's stay to a few weeks at the most.

Bradford Emergency Scheme

This scheme started in September 1977. Foster parents willing to receive children, who have to be received into care without prior notice, were recruited. Most of the children placed have been under the age of ten years and placings have averaged about four each week. The foster parents aim to offer intensive help to children whose previous material and emotional care may have been inadequate. Very recently, experience has shown that this emergency scheme can extend to older children, aged 15 or 16 years, and especially to girls of this age. Placements last for a few days only; usually the maximum stay is ten days. During this time, very good physical care is given high priority but emotional demands are kept at a low level. Experience, so far, suggests that if a placement is extended, then both the child and the foster parents begin to feel some emotional pressure. The advantage of this scheme is regarded by Bradford as offering less disruption to the life of a children's home, which can then concentrate on skilled longer term care, as well as less disruption in the life style of the individual child.

At this stage only experienced foster parents have been recruited for this emergency work. They receive the normal allowances but, in addition, a retainer fee of £10 is paid when the placement is not in use. One of the administrative problems foreseen is that of ending the arrangement when either the department or the family wishes to terminate the retained status.

Coventry Emergency Fostering Placement Scheme

This scheme started in November 1977 with six sets of foster parents. Children are placed in foster homes rather than residential establishments if they have to be received into care outside office hours. The foster homes receive children aged 0-17. If a teenage child is likely to be particularly difficult he is admitted to a residential establishment rather than to a foster home. Where possible, families of children are kept together.

The emergency foster parents keep children for up to two weeks. This period was determined by statistical analysis which showed that 35 per cent of children coming into care in fact returned home within two weeks. If this period is exceeded, the social workers make more permanent arrangements.

Foster parents work on a duty rota basis to cover out-of-office hours. The week is divided into nine sessions: Monday to Friday 5.00pm to 8.30am Saturday and Sunday 8.30am to 5.00pm, and 5.00pm to 8.30am. A payment of £3.50 is made for each session on duty whether or not the foster home is used, plus the normal maintenance payments made for foster children. Foster homes agree to take a minimum of two children each. Telephones are provided, if required, and telephone rentals are paid by the authority.

It is hoped to extend the scheme up to ten fostering couples with two sets of foster parents always in reserve. It is intended, as the scheme develops, that foster parents should work in teams of two living close to each other. Foster parents in the scheme may be used when not on duty if a large family has to be received into care.

Chapter 4
Fostering in transition

Traditional fostering

This report emphasizes experiments and new initiatives. In so doing, it inevitably minimizes the changes in traditional fostering. Without some reference to these, an unbalanced picture would result. A very few agencies, mainly in rural areas, indicated that they continued to find enough foster homes relatively easily but did not comment on the categories of children to be fostered. Traditional and 'exclusive' rural fostering was playing a smaller part in the whole fostering programme.

What is traditional fostering? As a rough and ready definition, it might be described as caring for a child within a family, accepting the child as one of the foster family, accepting payment to cover expenses and not demanding or being required to undertake training. This inquiry indicated that the development of special schemes had had a ripple effect on all forms of fostering and that there was a tendency to develop fostering as a many-stranded-activity.

Manchester, which has used special foster homes since 1969, accepted an overall total of 86 new foster families in 1974–75 but inceased the number of acceptance to 102 families in 1976–77. Coventry, which has a Family Life for Young People scheme linked to an Intermediate Treatment programme, is using foster parents for observation and assessment of all children under the age of seven years, and increased its total foster placements from 23 per cent in March, 1974 to 36 per cent in June 1977. Lewisham which started recruiting for hard-to-place children in 1974, found that, by the autumn of 1977, nearly all children under the age of 11 years, including mentally handicapped children, for whom fostering was considered appropriate, could be placed in families. Newcastle significantly increased family placement for short and long stay children who showed great variety in their needs, by investing heavily in individual and group support to foster parents, whether or not they happened to have a child in placement.

Taking the picture as a whole, fostering is now so diversified and dynamic that it is questionable whether 'traditional', 'special' or 'professional' should be regarded as other than developments towards a clearer definition of tasks.

Those who regard professional or special fostering as a distinction without a difference, point to the commonality of values and commitment in all forms of fostering and see the current stage as transitional. In regarding foster children as part of the foster family for as long as necessary, they assert that traditional fostering now provides care and affection rather than possessive love and does not usurp the legal rights or major decision making functions that properly belong to the natural parents or the placement agency. They assume that many foster parents, but not all, will tend to subscribe in general to the aims of NFCA. They suggest that the foster parents' function and role are precisely understood and clarified in short stay fostering; that they are less clear in intermediate fostering although becoming better understood as a result of more task centred case work aimed at goals specified in a contract; and that they are least clear in long term placements. The lack of clarity in long term placements relates to the equivocal position of the child and his natural family, to obstacles in planning the child's future and to the potential for the development of close emotional ties away from the natural family.

Traditional fostering has included the acceptance of some handicapped, particularly educationally subnormal children, and has offered care to children from different ethnic groups. Holman (Holman, 1973, and 1975) drew attention to this variety in fostering while noting that maladjusted children seemed infrequently to be found in foster homes. Traditionally fostering has tended to be a resource mainly for young children, partly for demographic reasons and partly to provide for emotional bonds early in life. Yet traditional fostering had been so multi-purpose, so flexible and so imprecise in terms of rewards sought and given, that many question why special or professional schemes have had to be invented except to point up, in dramatic form, the needs and services due to all foster parents.

Against these views, there are voiced arguments that traditional fostering has been constrained by regulatory control; over-restricted to care, substitute parenting and voluntary service. Some of the newer developments are seen as different because they offer a treatment resource, an occupation for reward and the use of fostering for specific and time limited purposes. A policy of family placement for adolescents direct from home or from residential care is seen as a new development.

Regulations

Developments in fostering have now moved beyond some of the procedural requirements imposed by the *Boarding-out of Children Regulations,* England and Wales, 1955, and Scotland, 1959. These apply both to statutory and to voluntary agencies but now seem unduly restrictive and out of tune with current social attitudes. While allowing children with physical and mental handicaps to be boarded out with foster parents, the regulations were promulgated when healthy young children were regarded as those most suitable for family placement. However, the myth grew that children had to be medically 'fit for adoption' or 'fit for boarding out'. But since the fifties medical and technological advances have helped some severely handicapped adults and children to function more adequately. In addition concern has grown about the need for handicapped children to experience family rather than hospital or residential care. Currently some agencies have a more comprehensive approach to children's needs and a positive attitude towards family placement for children who may have severe medical and handicapping conditions. It is increasingly recognised that many of these children should have permanent emotional ties as well as good physical care.

The existing regulations restrict fostering to certain family situations which include a married couple acting jointly, a woman or certain nominated male relatives. But family life styles have been diversified since the fifties by the steady growth in the number of women in employment outside the home, by the increase in marriage breakdowns and re-marriages and by the introduction of immigrant patterns of family relationships. The 1959 Scottish regulations do not permit a foster parent to depend for a living mainly on payments received from fostering but, since then, such a restriction has been called into question by the development of salaried or fee paid fostering. Other than in exceptional circumstances, geographical restrictions, included in both sets of regulations, inhibit the placement of a child in the care of a Scottish agency being fostered south of the border and a child from England or Wales being placed in Scotland. This inhibition can be a barrier in home finding for hard-to-place children.

The regulations formally and legally put the power to place and remove a child from a foster home upon the placement agency's representative. Developments in fostering practice, while recognising agency responsibility and public accountability, have moved in the direction of perceiving fostering as a more participative and shared task which respects the rights and responsibilities of natural and foster parents, children and agencies. The question now is whether it continues to be realistic to entrust a twenty-four-hour responsibility to foster parents while authority and responsibility remain so completely vested in the agency. One of the central principles of the Children Act, 1975, was the welfare of the child and his right to express his wishes and feelings. Any new regulations will need to reflect this emphasis on the right of the child.

A further problem posed by regulations, unmodified for 30 years, is that the formal 'undertaking' to be signed by foster parents for long term placements was and is a once-and-for-all document which, apart from being easily lost because it had no continuing function, firmly placed foster parents in a substitute parenting role. This role can be highly confusing now that patterns in fostering have become so diverse.

The case for updating the regulations is strong on historical and practical grounds and is under consideration in England and Wales.

One question is why fostering should be so closely regulated when the position of other vulnerable clients who may increasingly make use of family placement is not. Like children, elderly, physically frail and confused people also have dependency needs and are exposed to financial exploitation, neglect, ill treatment and indignity.

A second question is whether detailed procedures having the force of law produce dynamic practice or promote development.

A third question is whether adequate safeguards can be provided by regulations, guidelines or a framework embracing concepts of shared care applicable to a variety of day or residential family placements.

The general impression gained from respondents to this inquiry was that a safety net was important and there should be some basic national requirements to protect the rights of all parties to a family placement but a guideline, rather than a regulatory approach, was favoured as likely to be more productive of responsible, safe and reliable practice. Those who favoured a guideline approach saw the restrictive regulations as a clumsy instrument for organising a set of sensitive human relationships. Avoidance of the regulations, resorted to in order to secure a satisfying relationship in what might have seemed an unorthodox situation some thirty years ago, caused considerable anxiety to agencies and practitioners but 'getting round the regulations' seemed, in every discussion, to be a necessary activity because they no longer fitted the current scene. How to promote new developments and reconcile acceptance of new family life styles within the regulations was diverting energy and causing conflict and concern to local policy makers and practitioners. The development of freelance and salaried fostering schemes is beyond the concept of the regulations.

Freelance or salaried foster services

Responses to this inquiry showed that the large majority of existing and proposed schemes for fostering special categories of children were based on freelance, fee-for-service arrangements which resembled a self-employment situation. Those in favour of these schemes suggested that:

1. choice, negotiability and room to manoeuvre were preserved for all parties and these conditions were particularly important in the case of older children who were actively involved in decision making and attainment of agreed goals;
2. adjustments could be made to accommodate changes in the foster parents' own family situation and life style by means either of rest periods or the acceptance of a more limited or more complex task or category of child;
3. power, status and colleagueship were attained by the foster parents through exercising skill and gaining experience so that they could increasingly accept responsibility for and come to terms with the success and

failure of placements over which they had exercised some initial control;
4. freelance status conferred bargaining rights and influence which enabled the foster parents to act as advocates for the child and for themselves;
5. freelance status was higher than the status accorded by bureaucratic organizations to their lowly paid salaried foster parent employees.

The smaller number of agencies which favoured salaried schemes suggested that:
1. foster parents and agency had the advantage of predictable and guaranteed resources;
2. the benefits of regular employment and agreed conditions of service conferred rights on the foster parents and obligations on the agency and these could be established on a contractual basis;
3. the occupational status of the foster parents was clarified within the agency by virtue of their status as employees;
4. foster parents automatically acquired the benefit of training, access to records and the services provided by the agency for all its staff;
5. the formalised role and task of salaried foster parents were more acceptable to natural parents who tended to feel at a disadvantage when interacting with freelance foster families;
6. the colleagueship relationship with social workers and related professionals was facilitated by regular employment.

Some of these arguments cancelled each other out. On the whole, it seemed that freelance schemes were preferred partly because fostering has traditionally been a home based industry, partly because the newer models imported from Europe and North America tended to be free lance but mainly because convenience and flexibility were inherent in them. But little appeared to be known about the reactions of children and natural parents who, in the face of the publicity attaching to these schemes, cannot continue in ignorance of the reward and conditions of service elements in them. Consumer research may become important if these developments are to proliferate.

Basic fostering rates
The inquiry revealed concern at variations in basic fostering rates. Opinion was expressed that fostering could not significantly develop until basic rates and allowances increased in some parts of the country. One agency, after comparing its rates with those paid by its neighbours in 1975, found that it had underestimated the payments to long-stay foster parents by 80 per cent of the actual cost. Another agency, following a review, decided to reach NFCA recommended rates in four stages of planned expenditure. In addition to the variations in basic rates, discretionary payments had proved to be so complex as to be a burden to foster parents, to social workers and to administrators. The whole payment system was seen as too complex and therefore detrimental to effective publicity and recruitment. The extreme variations in basic rates and allowances have been exposed recently in

answer to a question in the House of Commons (*Hansard,* 14.2.78).

A major issue is whether a national basic foster rate should be adopted or whether the present variations which reflect local priorities and local costs should be continued. The system of agencies fixing a basic weekly rate, normally paid in arrears, supplying equipment and making additional discretionary payments for extras such as holidays, gifts, special clothing and individual requirements has developed into a miniature social security and supplementary benefit system. It has also generated tax problems.

Recently small gains have been made here and there. A few agencies now pay for the first as well as the last day of placement instead of one or the other. At least one agency pays in advance instead of in arrears. Others have paid contributions towards telephones in emergency and in short-stay foster homes or when placements require immediate contact with the agency or other social and health services. Yet other agencies have made a special payment for household help in preference to the use of the home help service. Apart from any statutory allowances, what is available for handicapped children under special or professional fostering schemes seems to be kept separate from any provisions which might equally be available to them under the Chronic Sick and Disabled Persons Act, 1970.

NFCA has continued to press for a national basic rate indexed to the General Household Survey figures and annually reviewed. The Association of Directors of Social Services in England and Wales favours a national basic rate and the local authority associations are prepared to consider the question. The issue remains open:

Is a national basic rate desirable or is the clamour for a national rate an irritated reaction to the gross discrepancies among locally fixed rates and allowances?

Are regional agreements on basic rates to be preferred to one national rate because they make some allowance for differences in the cost of living in parts of the country? If so, why have they not been negotiated?

Is it desirable for national and local voluntary agencies to conform to national, regional or local rates or should the voluntary sector reach its own independent agreements?

Is fixing fostering rates mainly Regional Council and Local Authority husbandry? Should the associations of statutory authories take the lead in examining the current disparities and in negotiating settlements which overcome the extreme variations and produces greater equity?

Is reluctance to establish the rate for the job a factor in inflating the growth of 'professional' schemes which include a reward element?

Is it appropriate to make a payment which gives foster parents choice and control over expenditure so that they are free to pursue their own life style in their own way?

Is there a risk of creating a private sector model for family placement within the public sector?

Is it desirable to reduce the multiplicity of discretionary payments and to ensure that they are made public?

These questions are very relevant to the type, extent and effectiveness of publicity and recruitment. They are very relevant to the 'satisfied customer' image. The current variations and complexities were reported as a constant source of error in calculation leading to inequality and frustration among foster parents and agency staffs.

Questions about payments

The description of special fostering schemes given in this report quote the fees being paid during the Autumn of 1977. Although more recent adjustments may have been made, the variation in fees, as with the basic non-taxable allowances, was considerable. The variation was not explicable in terms of costs incurred by the agency or costs expected to be incurred by a family in relation to a particular child or a particular task. These and other factors had some influence on determining the amount of financial reward attached to a scheme.

The issue of payment, in excess of the normal allowances, and the effect upon agency budgets, upon traditional foster parents and upon residential social workers is controversial.

According to one view:

The reward was a recognition of skill, commitment to undertaking an agreed task and sticking with that task.

The reward was also a recompense for home based employment and might bear some comparison with earnings in outside employment. When the home based employment was stipendiary the salary could be related to an appropriate public sector scale. But the reward was unlikely to match earnings which could be gained elsewhere and was unlikely to represent the sole motivation in fostering.

The fee or salary was offered as an inducement to people who possessed or might acquire the necessary skills to undertake difficult and demanding work within their own homes.

The skills rewarded might be described as parenting skills or as human relationship skills. The distinction may become important for calculating the amount of reward for parenting young, long term handicapped children or, alternatively, for offering human relationships to difficult adolescents for a short period.

Those who followed this line of thinking saw fostering for reward as skilled work in a particular setting and for selected children. They did not see it as a resource which was thought to be cheaper than and better than residential care since fostering was unlikely ever to be a universal panacea for all long stay children. The reward element was also seen as a payment for disturbance in the family's life and some recompense for the commitment made by all family members, especially natural children and husbands.

According to a second view:

Alleged cost saving, compared with residential care, was an attractive feature in selling schemes to policy makers and to the public.

Financial saving, even when a fee or salary was paid was an added virtue to the treatment of choice argument.

Family placement was better for the child and, fortunately cheaper too.

There was a marked absence of rigorous estimating or cost accounting by financial experts. This was partly because estimating the costs of new ventures is notoriously difficult and partly because the real costs of common support services, such as administrative and social worker time, were elusive and often ignored. Expert cost benefit analysis was not available. Authentic cost exercises which appeared more credible in the case of small, separately structured family placement units seemed to be based upon assumptions that the children placed in families would necessarily have remained in residential care until the age of 18. Until expert cost exercises have been completed for schemes of some duration, the purely financial advantage must remain an assumption. Nearly all the evidence given was in favour of the assumption being a correct one. While this may well be so, the issue is one for verification and for testing.

In the present state of knowledge about the effects of institutionalization, arguments for family placement rest rather more firmly on a treatment option basis than on financial grounds.

An area of confusion, complexity and concern, and one expressed by NFCA, is liability for taxation. Broadly, payments only become taxable when they represent income and reward in excess of necessary expenditure. Payments made in excess of the combined basic rates and some discretionary allowances for hard-to-place children or children with special needs for short term family life experiences are taxable. NFCA is negotiating with the Board of Inland Revenue on this issue. The evidence of this inquiry suggests that special schemes are proliferating and that it is urgent to clarify the tax situation. It is, however, appropriate to ask whether NFCA should negotiate or whether it is the paying agencies that should be concerned with negotiations. It is also appropriate to ask whether there are any grounds for tax exemption when a fee or salary is paid over and above necessary expenditure. On the other hand, can the fostering of hard-to-place and special need children ever be regarded as comparable with regulated employment?

Chapter 5
Adoption: a changing social pattern?

Adoption has been concerned with building new families mainly by placing illegitimate children as young as possible with childless couples. It has involved the legal severance of all ties with the family of origin. In the future adoption may well become an option whenever a child cannot realistically be brought up by his natural family. There will be choices but adoption will be appropriate for children drawn from a wider range who need the experience and security of life in a family able and willing to accept full responsibility. Adoption may be less frequently for the whole period of infancy to majority but more often for a shorter and later part of that total period. Given later adoption of children who automatically bring with them knowledge of their origins and the dignity of their own identity, the present secrecy, preserved by law, may through social custom become less usual. Older children, when adopted, may not always wish to change their surnames. Adoption may, like fostering, develop a variety of patterns which include familiar and, as yet, unfamiliar arrangements to suit a society in which marriage, divorce and remarriage coupled with economic vicissitudes demand new forms of legalised family attachments for children.

By way of example, figures supplied by the Church of England Children's Society for the last decade show that there has been a drop in the number of children placed (page 115) but that the Society has for many years placed children with special needs (*Table 6*). In any discussion of special need children there is a problem of definition. Every individual child has special needs but beyond these there are considerable differences in degree. These differences may range from minor to severe problems and disabilities. Some questions for the future will include:

Is adoption to include a wider age range of children?

Is adoption to include a wider range of categories of children?

Is adoption to be used more frequently when long term placement is inevitable?

Is adoption to be more frequently considered when, after a period of working towards rehabilitation with the natural family, restoration appears unlikely but parental consent is with-held?

Is the procedure for enabling parents to transfer parental rights and duties to an adoption agency to be used positively with adequate and skilled help for all those concerned?

Who is adoptable?

The Children Act, 1975, introduced a mechanism which, when implemented, may well have significant effect on planning for children unlikely to be brought up by their natural parents. The Act's provision for freeing a child for adoption is intended to secure early placement and reduce uncertainty where a deliberate decision to relinquish the child can be made early by the parents, and the child is placed or is likely to be placed for adoption. In Scotland, the child, if a minor, must also consent or be adjudged to be incapable of giving consent. The proposed mechanism can also be seen as recognition that time is of great significance in a child's healthy, emotional, physical and intellectual development. Decision making has already been shown, in the research studies referred to, to be crucial in family placement programmes (page 20). At the extreme, the view is expressed that no child is unadoptable. This view abandons the traditional rules of eligibility for adoption as far as children are concerned and no longer seeks the perfect child to meet the needs of a disappointed, childless couple. According to this view family placements should relentlessly be sought for children recognised as likely to present difficulties in rearing, to need very hard work in bringing up and to offer no guarantee of success, however defined. Couples, childless or not, who feel they have parenting and human relationship skills to offer complex children are seen as the future potential adopters. Among the children who may be placed for adoption are older children, sibling groups, mentally and physically handicapped children and emotionally damaged children who have lost their trust in human relationships and in the organizations that society creates. In essence, these children are all but indistinguishable from the group of hard-to-place children needing family life in foster homes but they are legally free, or have the prospect of becoming legally free, for adoption and may well have preferences of their own for a permanent new family. Barnardo's New Families Project and Parents for Children illustrate developments in these directions (pages 35 and 36).

Adoption for hard-to-place and special need children

Legal adoption for hard-to-place and special need children is as yet largely a matter of faith, belief and tentative experiment rather than of tested experience. But what experience there is suggests that whereas localisation can be regarded as a basic principle in many fostering schemes, adoptive homes for complex children have to be sought over a wide geographical area. The proliferation of resource exchanges is a recognition of this problem (pages 88 – 92). The possibility of approved adoption allowances is also a response to home finding, on a permanent basis, for these children.

Approved adoption allowances

If the number of hard-to-place and special need children who are adopted increases, and adopters are going to be involved in considerable expenditure on the children, the approval of adoption allowances, sometimes referred to as 'subsidised adoption', may well become a significant issue. This is not only because of the extra financial liabilities but also because the attention needed by some children is likely to preclude the wife from seeking employment outside the home. Further, without some allowance, a family whose income is already low for its own needs could find difficulty in taking on extra responsibilities. The Children Act, 1975, restricts payments to adopters by requiring schemes to be submitted to the Secretary of State for approval. Some agencies are considering forms of payment which would avoid a reduction in the family's normal standard of living or cover special and expensive provision for a particular child or group of children. ABAFA will shortly be making suggestions about circumstances likely to need approved adoption allowances.

Some principles, which raise controversial issues, have already reached the discussion stage and include a lump sum or a time-limited annual payment to families or for children, for example:

To adopters whose financial position is restricted until they are established in their business or profession; students whose training may extend to five or more years; families who need to buy a larger house; and couples where the wife may need to cease employment at least for a period in order to work with the adopted child;

To a family living permanently on a low income, such as families following a traditionally low paid vocation or drawing a variable income from the creative arts; and families whose income is reduced by disablement or whose work prospects are uncertain in a period of high unemployment;

To families whose financial and time commitments to other relatives (elderly parents) preclude them from adopting unless extra services and transport are paid for;

For individual children with disabilities or disease of a severe and possibly permanent nature needing additional expenditure on travel, holidays, household maintenance over and above generally available allowances, aids and equipment;

For individual children with rare gifts or talents which are likely to remain undeveloped without extra expenditure, effort and modification of a family's life style;

To family groups of children needing to be kept together.

In these examples, the payment of allowances relates either to the family circumstances or to the specific characteristics and needs of the adoptive children. Allowances are seen as relating to anticipated and justifiable expenditure of a kind that public opinion may find acceptable though not without careful explanation.

Perhaps even more controversial would be schemes which included allowances where adoption did not involve the complete severance of all natural family links but adoption, rather than custodianship, was in the interest of the child and of his first and new family.

There is also the issue of existing foster parents who wish to adopt a foster child but who cannot afford to do so. Natural families find children expensive and envy of financial gain, even though misconceived, could readily distort community attitudes and support for approved allowances unless there is full communication and understanding among foster parents, adopters and the general public.

Chapter 6
Some organizational and policy questions

The issues of policy and practice so far discussed affect organizational patterns and procedures for policy making. Nearly all agencies whether statutory or voluntary gave detailed information about organizational patterns. Responsibility for management, organizational and policy proposals was vested at assistant director level in more than one-third of the local authorities. In all but a few cases, the assistant director for fieldwork services was responsible. The variants included assistant directors for children's services, for field and domiciliary services, for home finding, for community services, for residential services; and in one case an assistant director for programme and research development and in another case a group leader for child, family and psychiatric services. In just under one-quarter of the authorities, the level was that of principal officer. Among the other authorities, about a dozen in all, responsibility was assigned either to the deputy director or to a professional consultant. The latter was outside the management hierarchy and exercised influence rather than power in advising management on policy and social workers on practice.

There appeared to be no direct relationship between organizational model and type or size of authority. In general, it seemed that the higher the level of responsibility, the greater the emphasis on a co-ordinating function and on maintaining links with other aspects of service delivery. It did not appear that, in itself, the level of highest responsibility was always the most influential in developing a lively placement policy. Charismatic leaders and active professional groups established to promote and implement policies and projects achieved thrust provided that they had elected member and managerial support. The problem that caused concern was how best to provide an organizational system which offered a wide range of services to families and at the same time to promote excellence in the practice of family placement without being over-zealous in its cause.

It was common practice for all divisions, areas and districts of social service departments to be involved in fostering in all its forms. This arrangement was less common in relation to adoption which, for historical reasons, remained an option for the few and still showed a tendency to be separately organized.

Three main patterns not always mutually exclusive could be distinguish ed to enable management to develop policy and practice. For simplicity, the term 'area' is used to denote localised units of service delivery; strict accuracy would require constant discrimination between division, area and district:

1. just over half the statutory agencies had adopted a representational system. Fostering was an area team responsibility but was supported by a super-structure. This super-structure was frequently composed of area or divisional directors, where the latter existed, and senior management staff and advisers or specialist assistants based at the agency's headquarters. Generally the super-structure was responsible for making policy proposals, ensuring the sharing of fostering resources, equalising opportunities for placement, developing practice and supporting experiment. But it was the area teams which implemented policy and practice;

2. in about one-third of the statutory agencies, there was a combined operation system. Responsibility for generating policy and development was shared. These authorities had specialist officers, usually senior social workers, based at headquarters and working with a principal officer to manage external relationships, to advise on practice and provide information to colleagues in area teams. The specialised groups at headquarters were nearly always very small. In some cases, the small groups appeared to have been inherited from former children's departments, but, in other instances, they were of recent origin, and sometimes matched by similar small teams concerned with developing service for other client groups;

3. in about a quarter of the statutory agencies there was a project or development unit at headquarters which in some cases existed in addition to the first two patterns. These units tended to be of very recent origin and to have executive as well as advisory functions. They were promoting newer forms of fostering rather than traditional practices throughout the agency or were managing small projects. To some extent, they were trouble-shooters and innovators.

In over a quarter of all statutory agencies, specialist fostering and/or adoption officers had been appointed in each division or area. These specialist social workers were usually appointed at senior social worker level. There were also many examples of informal nominations of an experienced worker or one who wished to develop a particular interest in family placement. There was still a tendency for family placement to attract or be undertaken by women workers employed on a part-time basis.

In Scotland, elected members and officers frequently shared the tasks of a working party. In England and Wales, working parties, liaison groups and case committees rarely included either elected members or representatives of voluntary agencies or of other related disciplines such as medicine and law. Overall policy and new developments in policy were proposed for approval first by the departmental management team and then by elected members.

Promotion of an active family placement policy clearly involved sharing of children and placements across divisions or areas. The mechanism to achieve this sharing did not operate without tensions. Reciprocity, exchange and barter across a whole range of resources was required. Questions may need to be asked by each agency about the effectiveness of the pattern selected to fit its particular circumstances. Decisions to set up specialist development teams or project groups may be a way of creating experimental capacity within the organization. In such situations questions arose about the autonomy of area teams, accountability and division of tasks.

But whatever the system chosen, the interest was in such questions as:

1. *whether management* was supplied with regular, accurate and detailed information about the child population needing family placement, the length of stay in care, the quality of relationship with the natural family and the process of planning and decision taking?

2. *whether resources* for family placement were being stock-piled and lost through delay, lack of decision-making or under-use; whether the placement families were receiving adequate service at all stages from initial inquiry to completion of placement?

3. *whether there was* regularly available a profit and loss account which revealed gains and losses to children and families?

4. *whether information* was collected about staff capacity, attitudes and ideas;

5. *whether advertisements* were being issued when unused foster homes were waiting in ignorance of the agency's special needs.

Patterns of organization

The following arguments were advanced in support of *localised,* area-based family placement services:

Short-stay fostering should cause the least disruption in the child's relationship with family and local community services. Home finding should increasingly be neighbourhood based, incorporate a self-help element and develop a community work approach. For example, Durham's Parent Teacher Association/Community Fostering Project was developed, during the summer of 1977, to involve PTAs in the statutory, or private, foster care of children attending a local school with a view to members of the PTA providing short-term foster care.

Assessment of family needs, including those of the children, should rely on local knowledge and help should be available from the local services common to all client groups.

From this perspective, centralisation should be regarded as philosophically and practically alien to the current pattern of family based and accessible personal social services. This perspective was typical of agencies which delegated authority but provided a highly skilled advisory service.

Such localisation should avoid the risks of over direction, whether pro-decural or professional, of elitism and of a return to unnecessary separation experiences for children and natural parents.

Further, provided there was ready access to expert and multi-disciplinary advice, localisation should reduce tensions between central and local staff.

The case for a *central unit* tended to lay greater emphasis on fostering and adoption as an integrated family placement service and stressed that:

A specialist team should boost recruitment and speed placement by concentrating on the regular examination of numbers and biographies of all children in the care of the agency as a whole and, preferably, in conjunction with other local and national agencies.

Foster and adoptive families needed support while awaiting placement as well as during one. Families and children lost out when the placement could not be made at the moment of readiness but such immediacy and depth of work could not be expected of local generic teams with their variety of daily pressures and conflict of interests. This argument could be called the 'Families Cannot Wait' concept.

Foster homes, short or long-stay, were a resource for the whole agency and some mechanism was needed to equalize opportunities among the divisions and areas to ensure the sharing of homes and optimum choice for children. Without such pressure from the centre, families and children remained for far too long in cold storage.

The greater the emphasis on family placement policy, the greater was the need for a task force operation to provide a knowledge and skill bank as a resource for development and experiment.

The need was for a highly skilled team to develop practice in homefinding and placement for children with special needs until such time as this type of placement became standardised practice.

There were other considerations which made a decision between varying degrees of central or local autonomy either more or less appropriate to a particular agency. Geography and demography were relevant. Some localities produced foster homes and few children needing care, while others, within the same agency, produced a high ratio of children but few placement families. This phenomenon applied both to statutory and voluntary agencies. Another factor was the number of voluntary agencies within the boundaries of a statutory authority, whether or not they undertook both fostering and adoption, and the extent to which agencies were prepared to share out resources. Fewer than a dozen statutory authorities had made arrangements for adoptions to be entirely undertaken by a voluntary body. Organizational patterns were also affected by elected member pressures in favour of a family placement policy or by powerful professional interests at the centre or in the divisions or areas. In other cases, the sheer pressure of numbers of children being received into care and requiring urgent placement had markedly influenced the setting up of a central unit with some executive functions in addition to advisory ones. There was great variety in the patterns of organizations but one, devised by Coventry, is quoted here. The specialist workers in fostering and adoption are divided between the central Adoption and Fostering Unit and the fieldwork teams, but the functions of the unit are defined as follows:

1. to recruit and assess prospective adopters and foster parents;
2. to arrange the placement of children with long term substitute families;
3. to provide training for foster parents;
4. to provide, in conjunction with the principal training officer, training for staff wishing to undertake adoption and fostering work;
5. to promote and implement new fostering schemes;
6. to provide counselling for adopted people seeking their original birth certificates;
7. to advise staff at all levels on matters relating to fostering and adoption.

On the other hand, a few units had wider responsibilities for developing a programme for all services for children and families. These more widely based responsibilities might include measures for the prevention of child abuse, child minding services and alternatives to reception into care or managing both family and residential placements under a joint programme to ensure individual planning for each child. A further variation was for some units to concentrate on expanding placements outside the agency's own territorial boundaries with the help of fostering and adoption resource exchanges. Another function of some central units was to provide social work support for practitioners involved in family placement.

Social work support

Experienced consultants and project leaders emphasized the importance, whatever organizational structure was chosen, of building in support for young practitioners and consultation for more experienced ones. Increasingly group work support was offered. Young social workers were seen to be vulnerable to the grief and separation experiences of children and parents, to the fear of failure and breakdown and the pain of the resulting emotional stress. Many of them, newly married or with young children of their own, found the family tensions, and sometimes violence, that they had to meet in their work a threat to their own stability. Unless they could share their emotional reactions to some of the painful situations that confronted them, they were themselves at risk. Young social workers whose own childhood and adolescent experiences were relatively recent could easily be over exposed to the emotional turmoil of children and families in crisis. Skilled professional support was regularly needed and had to be recognised as quite distinct from educational and training programmes. Family placement groups, whether advisory or executive, recognised this need. In the area teams it was expected that social workers would look to their seniors for support or, increasingly, to the appointed or nominated fostering officers. But how did these officers find support?

Is one-to-one support adequate or do agencies need to build in group support for social workers under stress?

Is the stress experienced by residential workers under-estimated when they use their knowledge and skill to prepare a child for family placement and often help in a crisis later on?

Research, policy and practice

Research, practice wisdom and social attitudes have all been shown, in this report, to be influential in the movement towards an active family placement policy. In replying to the questions about published, current and desired research, it was clear that agencies, including those which had carried out their own 'Children Who Wait' surveys, and there were about 20 of these, maintained a continued questioning about the reason for the children's separation from their own parents. Such questioning seemed to be essential for broad policy making and for decisions about individual care and treatment. The three major areas of interest for research related to detailed information about the size, nature and disposition of the population of children in care, the characteristics of foster and adoptive families and the predictors of success and failure in family placement, particularly those factors applicable to experimental projects.

Important studies have refined the profile of the child population needing service including that of family placement. The Scottish Social Work Services Group took the lead in sponsoring and financing two research studies. One, (Newman and Mackintosh, 1975) examined the residential provision for children in South East Scotland, the use being made of it and the developments needed. The second (Seed and Thompson, 1977) was an investigation into the use of residential and day care for children in the Highlands and Western Isles of Scotland. These studies collected the data needed for central and regional policy development. In a study (Portsmouth, 1973) of the high numbers of Portsmouth children in care, it was suggested that negative social conditions alone were not responsible for the high numbers; these were also influenced by the local authority's response.

A study by Dr. John Triseliotis, University of Edinburgh, is nearing publication. It relates to the experience of 40 young people who grew up in foster care and were placed before the age of nine and stayed in foster homes until the age of at least 16 years. Another study, from the same source, will contrast special need children placed for adoption with a group of children aged 20 to 21 years who grew up either in foster or in residential care so that comparisons can be made among three different types of care. This latter study has started but the data will not finally be collected until 1980.

A typical use of the research capacity of a local authority was to obtain more precise knowledge about fostering as a resource. Two examples are given.

Mid-Glamorgan: a study of foster parents' experience

In 1975 a sample number of foster parents were interviewed to discover whether foster parents were dissatisfied with any processes of the fostering system as it then operated. The objective was to identify and correct any areas of discontent so that recruitment of foster parents would increase and wastage of existing foster parents would decrease.

The conclusion drawn from the study was that the fostering system was then in serious need of attention. Several areas of discontent were identified and they included:

1. the length of time the foster parents had had to wait to be interviewed, to be accepted and to receive a placement;
2. anticipated problems in the role and legal position of foster parents;
3. insufficient preparation and information about allowances; the inadequacy of allowances; lack of information about entitlement to special allowances and the inhibitions about asking for them;
4. the irregularity of social workers' visits, the quality of support and the difficulty of contacting them when necessary;
5. the lack of medical information about children placed; the stigma of the then current fostering stereotype.

The area most needing attention was thought to be the status of foster parents. If fostering were to attain a more professional status and if foster parents were to be regarded as members of a team working for the good of the foster child, the deterrent of stigma might be removed. It seemed that the whole content of the fostering system, the financial and social work support made available to fostering logically depended upon the expectation held of fostering. Immediate recommendations were made to improve fostering policy and practice.

Cheshire: children in care survey

This survey on Cheshire children in care (McGrath, 1977) illustrated the connection between survey policy, practice and research. Children who had had a statutory review during a three month period in the Autumn of 1976 were included in the survey irrespective of whether they were living in residential establishments, in foster homes or in their own homes at the material time. The main objectives were to examine ways in which placements fell short of the 'ideal' and to consider whether existing resources could be more effectively used.

The results, in line with other studies, showed a high rate of fostering breakdown and a high percentage of children in residential care who could ideally be fostered. It was recommended that the reasons for breakdown should be investigated and that adequate social work support was essential if fostering were to be expanded. The main obstacles, apart from lack of suitable foster parents, were identified as the need to keep siblings together, the child's problems of adjustment, the child's behaviour and the natural parents' attitude towards foster placement. These obstacles were thought to point to the expansion of traditional fostering and to the development of a special family placement project.

In general, there remains here and abroad, a lack of research about the effects of different kinds of treatment for children unable to live in their own homes and a lack of local, national and cross-cultural knowledge about the characteristics of families which are able to share their family life with children or others unrelated to them. It may well be that an important factor is the dearth of competent and sensitive research workers. Two final comments should be made about attitudes to research. A number of agencies expressed interest in finding out more about the factors conducive to success rather than to failure in fostering and adoption. Many voluntary adoption agencies regarded their records as valuable source material for research.

Chapter 7
Approaches to publicity and recruitment

Organizations which pursued an active family placement policy were much concerned with publicity. Traditional fostering and a regulatory approach have not, in the past, attracted aggressive publicity. Over two-thirds of all statutory and voluntary agency respondents gave information about publicity. The advocates of active publicity and vigorous family placement stressed that publicity required not only money but organizational competence to ensure a speedy response. A slow, uniformed show of interest or bureaucratic stalling were unproductive; what was needed was immediate response, prompt information giving, an invitation to an office interview or to an agency meeting or the promise of a home visit at a fixed time.

In this country, respect for identity and for confidentiality has traditionally imposed restraint upon personalised appeals. Publicity has been low key, disguised and related to a recognised category of children rather than to a recognisable child. The risk of embarrassment to child, natural family, foster parents or agency was thereby minimised. The 'satisfied customer' method of recruitment was regarded as reliable and safe. Successful and trusted foster parents were regarded as best suited to recruit others from their own social network and were thought of as offering a reliable recommendation for new recruits. This type of publicity still has its protagonists, particularly in rural areas, but it has the disadvantage of tending to recruit from a limited type of foster parent who resembles existing foster parents and is interested in traditional fostering.

Are conventional publicity methods effective when the ages and characteristics of the children needing family placement have changed?

Are special need children hard-to-place because they are not necessarily the choice of traditional foster parents?

Are children hard-to-place because their needs are not known to families interested in fostering and adoption?

From the early sixties, press advertisements which gave details, but no photographs, of individual children began to appear in newspapers and professional journals in an attempt to push fostering beyond traditional social class and geographic boundaries. Then, in the mid-sixties, the continuous, aggressive sales techniques used in the United States challenged traditional methods and British reticence when it was reported that real children were appearing on television and were involved in making direct appeals for family placement. At this time, the British Adoption Project sought and received active press interest. It broke the silence barrier around the healthy babies born in Britain of Asian, West Indian and mixed parentage who could be adopted. Since then co-operation between statutory and voluntary agencies and the media has increased. Voluntary organizations, particularly the large national ones, were at first more daring in using live children on television programmes. This was done only with the consent of the parent and child.

Replies to this inquiry showed that agencies which had a positive and promotional attitude towards publicity tended to centralise their management at headquarters. They had also developed close and trusting relationships with the press, television and radio.

Press, television and radio publicity

About 20 local authorities made active and regular use of the media for sustained publicity. They regarded the basic aim as raising the level of public consciousness about the needs of children in care rather than recruitment for family placement. In Scotland, particular projects and the S.E. Resource Centre made use of broadly based publicity. Agencies in London which had participated in the Soul Kids campaign (pages 76 and 77) to recruit black foster parents and those agencies which worked with Parents for Children and ARE deliberately committed themselves to following an activist policy of publicity for children with special needs. A handful of other agencies, widely scattered, made special arrangements with the media for recruitment publicity to accompany special projects mounted to find homes for hard-to-place children. Regular feature articles in weekly newspapers, describing individual children and showing their photographs, were used by a few authorities. Another small group of authorities circulated their own newspapers giving fostering news, pictures and detailed descriptions of children needing placement. How far it is ethical or effective to break confidentiality in order to secure family placement is still being debated. There is as yet no tested evidence that aggressive publicity produces satisfying family placement, but agencies which had used active publicity methods seemed satisfied that public awareness was being increased.

Dramatic presentation on the media was not the only innovation in publicity. Other examples quoted included a mobile bus for publicity purposes, a van in a market place and a market stall for information. Posters and exhibition material had been displayed in industrial premises, departmental stores, public houses and other key centres where people congregated. These initiatives had met with varying degrees of success; for example, a market stall was reported to be unsuccessful, but a manned display in a departmental store had produced serious interest. This current inquiry has produced little hard information about the effectiveness of different types of publicity. If this is to be tested, then the relationship between the type of publicity and the quality of response is the key question.

Keith Soothill, University of Lancaster, is producing a report on foster parent recruitment in parts of Lancashire. The report includes a description of various campaigns conducted over a two-year period, the procedure for approving applicants, the characteristics of those approved for fostering, the assessment of foster homes and follow up schemes. The long term difficulties of retaining foster parents will be studied subsequently.

National or local publicity

There was divided opinion as to whether publicity could be produced nationally for local use both by statutory and voluntary agencies. National publicity was held to be relatively inexpensive and useful as a saturation technique, but it quickly became outmoded and it did not speak to local cultures. Advocates of unremitting publicity who pinned their faith on locally produced material believed in the response of local loyalty to local need. Many local advertisements were dramatic in their presentation. Dorset announced its special fostering project 'PROJECT FOSTERING can bring your family up to £50 a week for working with adolescents. . .'. Bradford, in promoting a community parent scheme for teenage children who would otherwise live in residential care, adopted the slogan 'Earning a hundred and twenty pounds per month — the hard way'.

Views varied about the effectiveness of occasional publicity campaigns. Just under a dozen authorities relied on the occasional campaign which used both national and local publicity.

Lewisham has pursued an active recruitment policy which includes full participation in the 'Mums and Dads All London Fostering Campaign' of 1976 and 1977 (page 79) and has used active recruitment to emphasize, in particular, the need for black foster parents. Broadly based recruitment activity between September, 1975, and January, 1977, produced the following results: initial inquiries 224; applications pursued 153; applications closed 103; applications accepted 34; and applications pending 16.

About a dozen authorities had found the result of campaigns to be disappointing and had abandoned them. Another small group of authorities had specifically directed their publicity to particular localities in an attempt to work up interest in a neighbourhood. In 1976 a market research company conducted a study for the NFCA, with the co-operation of Coventry social services department, to evaluate the effectiveness of a recent foster parent recruitment campaign in the city. The central objective was to assess the reactions of potential recruits. The study gave an indication of the state of mind and needs of the potential recruits: some were very self-confident and sure of their desire to foster; many more were much less confident. Coventry considered that the study showed valuable insights into the different types of approaches needed to interest potential recruits.

With neither uniformity nor agreement about publicity there was great variety in practice and in the resources invested: from the 'satisfied customer' approach, through individual advertisement preserving anonymity, to individual appeal including a photograph, to aggressive publicity using the media and dramatic campaigns. American and to some extent British experience, of positive or aggressive and personalised publicity which reveals identity and abandons anonymity, has shown that some success can be achieved in finding family placements for children with very varying needs and from very varying situations. Details of the response to the Granada T.V. 'campaign' have been supplied by ARE (*Table 7*).

The 'end justifies the means' argument tends to be used to support aggressive publicity. Without it, some children would never achieve family placement. With it, sensibility may be offended, confidentiality breached and indignity suffered. This is essentially a moral decision.

Experience of working with hard-to-place children in America (Donley, 1975) and here in Kent, Lambeth and Wandsworth (to take three examples) suggests that new methods of announcing policies, giving information and describing the real needs of real children may be necessary to interest families who have something they wish to give to a handicapped child or families who wish to supplement their income by working with complex and older children at home. The second motivation requires official recognition of payment for home-based employment. Yet other families have an ideological, religious or humanitarian concern which they wish to express in caring for, say, black or mixed race children in order to give tangible expression to non-racial attitudes. The question is how these groups of people in the community can be alerted to the actual needs, by what method and for what categories of children without, at the same time, losing the contribution of traditional foster parents, with their own idealism of non-profit making community service for fostering children some of whom have also been very demanding in their needs.

Choices have to be made about publicity which can be expensive in money and manpower.

Should publicity first be aimed at community education as an essential precursor to recruitment before being used for recruiting?

Should an informed public then be introduced to the needs and characteristics of target groups within the local population of children in care?

Is aggressive publicity an American import unsuited to the cultural habit of understatement in this country?

How do children in care and natural parents view aggressive and personalised publicity?

Adoption publicity

Whether publicity was regular and relentless or restrained and muted, it was mainly directed towards fostering. In relation to adoption, publicity was only used when seeking families to adopt children with special needs. The local well-established voluntary agencies which still had open lists for young white babies continued to rely upon the communication network within their own religious affiliations and subscribers, their annual meetings and occasional social functions. Indirectly, some of them participated in more activist publicity arranged by Adoption Resource Exchanges. Active publicity was an important preliminary approach used by some of the more recently established voluntary agencies geared to finding adoptive homes for hard-to-place children.

Home finding for black children

Black people are concentrated in some of the major industrial connurbations. 'Black' is used here to refer to non white people as a shorthand method of referring collectively to members of minority groups as a category separate from the white host community. In some urban areas, black children may form a significant proportion of the population of children in care though they may not all necessarily require long term care. Nonetheless, when they do, they often feature among the 'children who wait' population in both the statutory and voluntary sectors. Efforts to find family placements for them have characterised some national and local publicity campaigns. These have included efforts to recruit foster parents from minority groups despite difficulties which may be occasioned by housing problems, by low income and by single parent family patterns in some groups and by the general stress of adaptation to a different culture and life style. The situation was reviewed in *Fostering Black Children* in 1975 (CRC, 1975). In addition to the expansion of day facilities, a need was seen for the standard of care given to privately fostered children to measure up to that of the statutory and voluntary fostering services, for liaison fostering officers to be appointed in social service departments covering areas where over ten per cent of births were to black people and for increasing the understanding of social workers about the particular problems and sensitivities of black children, especially during adolescence. The need for professional status and supplementary allowances to facilitate the recruitment of black people as foster parents was also stressed.

The Commission for Racial Equality (the new body which replaces the Community Relations Commission) is considering the production of basic leaflets for distribution to minority groups interested in fostering or adoption. It already publishes information pamphlets about the diet, customs, habits and cultural patterns of the main minority groups. Some Community Relations Councils are actively trying to recruit foster parents from minority groups but the degree to which this is done varies from area to area and relationships between the Councils and agencies vary. From the Commission's view point, the need is for workers, not necessarily social workers but those from a community work or other appropriate background, to reach out to the black children and families through knowledge, understanding and appreciation of their cultural heritage and background.

In publicity, which aims at family placement for black children, the inclusion of black children somewhat indiscriminately among disturbed, disruptive or handicapped children may cause resentment. It may be a matter of some consequence to avoid publicity which, through lack of knowledge or understanding, inadvertently appears insensitive and counter productive for recruitment purposes. In recruiting black foster parents practical support and regular payments, equivalent to a salary, may be essential for some families where, for economic reasons, the wife normally seeks outside employment. For example, it is common practice for West Indian wives to work outside the home. Whilst the Commission recognises that black children may need to be placed in families, whether for fostering or adoption, which are of a different racial background, it is anxious to increase recruitment of black families for black children. One experiment mounted by nine London Boroughs in 1975 illustrated some of the problems, misunderstandings and possibilities. This project was known as the 'Soul Kids Campaign'.

A number of agencies have made special efforts over recruitment for family placement for black children. On 30th September, 1975, black children represented 37.2 per cent of all children in the area of Lewisham but 42.5 per cent of all children who were fostered. Many of these children were in short stay care. From a broader base, it seems important for agencies to develop close relationships with different ethnic groups in order to develop family placement arrangements which are understood and appreciated.

Chapter 8
Proposed developments and innovations

The aspirations of respondents ranged from a gleam-in-the-eye to a proposed plan for 1978. Their expressed ambitions have been classified and ranked in a descending order of popularity. They relate mainly to local authorities and to the national rather than the local voluntary agencies.

Special schemes attracting a financial reward
Some 30 local authorities and the major voluntary organizations were interested in or intending to develop fostering schemes, mainly for adolescents, as an alternative or supplement to residential care, and based on a contract to achieve selected treatment goals. Four are quoted but it should be recorded that a few respondents expressed reservations about special schemes and preferred not to join the 'bandwagon' until more evaluation was available.

Cheshire Family Placement Project
The Cheshire Family Placement Project was planned in 1977 in anticipation that placements would start during March, 1978. The objective is to recruit lay people who, in their own homes, can provide effective help to children and young persons who have severe problems of social adjustment and must leave home, at any rate, for a short period. The belief is that, given the right kind of support and incentive, families are able to carry out tasks which have traditionally been assigned to professionals. The hope is that more effective help is obtained for such children if as much money is spent on developing family placement in the community as it costs to use a place in a residential establishment.

The principles underlying the project include the child's right to a normal home life, involving the use of all ordinary community facilities, and the recognition that the child and his family should agree with and participate actively in decisions concerning them. The project thus presupposes community based rather than institutional care and treatment, and the creation of a new resource option. The dynamics of the project depend on keeping the basic issues as simple and explicable as possible. Planning, treatment and methods are intended to emphasize the child's conscious and recognisable needs and to respond with positive practical and achievable treatment objectives.

Inclusion of a child in family placement presupposes the existence and awareness of a crisis on the part of the child and his family and their ability and motivation to effect change for the better. Problems presented by youngsters are varied but their impact on those around them tends to be great whether it be a single major problem or a collection of problems made impressive by their numbers. The connecting threads tend to be some very unsatisfactory experiences in basic upbringing and serious difficulties in relating to people whether adults or peers. Referrals for placement may originate in various ways; e.g., from case conferences or reviews held in a residential centre, school or child guidance clinic or as a consequence of multi-disciplinary involvement in Intermediate Treatment group work.

The project family represents the 'front line' for treatment and resources. Their relationship with the child or young person will be based on the achievement of treatment objectives rather than that of substitute parenting, even though the provisions of good physical and emotional care is essential. A disciplined understanding will be the prerequisite to the project family's professional role. Professionalism in this context implies commitment to and ability to work with project objectives and methods, rather than formal qualifications. Commitment involves attendance at project family group meetings for training, professional support, and influence over policy development and membership of a professional team.

A fee of £35 per week will be paid in respect of each child placed in addition to the normal fostering allowances and both will be subject to annual review. No precise age limits for placement have been laid down, but certain features of the scheme, such as the contractual arrangements, favour older children. Only in exceptional circumstances will more than two children be placed concurrently with the same project family. Where a child stays on with a family beyond the 'contract' stage which means beyond the termination of the treatment plan, only the normal fostering allowance will be paid. A retainer fee of £17.50 per week, but no fostering allowance, will be paid at the end of a placement provided the family is willing to undertake a further placement. Travelling allowances will be payable. The contract will require a minimum of one month's notice on either side. For the purposes of household insurance, family placement is likely to be treated as 'fostering on a commercial basis'. However, the authority is negotiating a special policy to cover those who take children under the terms of this project. The fee paid to a project family is likely to be taxable and negotiations are being undertaken with the Inland Revenue and guidance will then be issued to project families about tax returns.

Lewisham Teenage Placements

This proposed scheme is intended to succeed an earlier scheme for hard-to-place children which started in 1974 and has maintained four mentally handicapped children in long stay foster homes. After a survey of children in long term care, Lewisham is now proposing home finding for:

1. a group of 11–13 year-old children who have spent time in residential care and are thought to need family care to help them during adolescence;
2. some children of 14 years and over with behaviour problems who have lived in residential care for several years, and need family life and a therapeutic situation;
3. a few children who have been living at home but need a special placement including some who might be placed directly after a court appearance.

The proposal involves a specially prepared advertisement campaign and a fee of £25 which will continue to be paid as a retainer between placements.

Norfolk Family Care Project

The project is aimed at testing out whether some adolescents could be transferred from residential care to live in families. The pilot scheme is managed by the area fostering officer and is limited to one area of the county, but, if found satisfactory will be extended to others.

A phased operation lasting seven months has been planned from August, 1977, to early Spring, 1978. This plan starts with communications within the department and extends to involvement of existing foster parents to avoid misunderstandings, work with residential establishments, identification of children, recruitment of foster parents, training in groups, selection oɪ applicants, and finally placement. Such a time scale was a fairly representative one but staff changes could cause severe slippage and many respondents noted this.

The proposed fee is £35 weekly in addition to the fostering rates normally applicable to the particular adolescent. At the recruitment stage, 25 inquiries had been received; and five couples had started and four couples had completed a training course.

Barnardo's Home Care Scheme: Edinburgh

This project which is expected to start in the summer of 1978 will aim at family placement for disturbed and maladjusted children referred for residential care, but unsuited or unlikely to benefit from treatment in a residential group situation until some of their basic needs for individual care have been met. The children will be too disturbed for traditional foster parents. Most of the children will retain their own family ties and will need treatment to meet their special emotional demands and to modify their behaviour patterns.

The proposal is to recruit families, as an extension of residential provision, who are willing to work in a parent/therapist role, on a time-limited basis of six months to two years, with the child and with the natural family where appropriate.

This will be a salaried employment scheme for the foster mother, or exceptionally the foster father. Salary will be a non-incremental scale of

£1884 per annum, plus cost of living supplements, but payments will include the tax free element of the usual fostering rate, and will attract superannuation, insurance, sickpay, holidays with pay and the usual service conditions of public employment.

The project's senior social worker will have a professional support group and will be responsible for co-ordinating the work with the therapy family and the natural family and for any review of the treatment goals. To achieve its aims, the project will be localised and seen as a potential resource for the Lothian social work department. Without counting Barnardo's management and administrative costs, which will be regarded as their 'voluntary contribution', the estimated costing of the actual work with the child and both families is about £64 per week.

Adoption

More than twenty local authorities wished to give some priority to adoption and to develop a comprehensive service when resources permitted. The contribution to be made by the statutory and voluntary sectors for such a service had not been worked out in any detail but the Department of Health and Social Security is hoping to mount a project with Bedfordshire and Newcastle local authorities in conjunction with local voluntary adoption agencies. It is recognised that adoption is likely to be increasingly concerned with older children and with a wider range of children.

The influence of the Children Act, 1975, of ABAFA and of ARE is evident in attitudinal and practice changes. Counselling for adults remains highly specialised because of its comparative rarity. A few adoption agencies, for example, Edinburgh Guild of Service, Doncaster Adoption and Family Welfare Society, Dundee Association for Social Services and Chichester Diocesan Association, have already started to experiment with making contact with adopters and adoptees some time after the court order has been made. There has been an unexpectedly high response to these approaches.

Voluntary organizations have sponsored free and confidential advice to people who find it difficult to approach formal agencies. A 'phone-in' service started in Surrey and Sussex in 1976 and from November 1977 it was extended to cover more new areas from Greater London to the Isle of Wight. There have been experiments in other parts of the country but usage has been variable.

A confidential counselling service for anyone with any problems relating to adoption was launched by Barnardo's Yorkshire divisional office in 1975 (Smith, 1976). The advice sought concerned many aspects of adoption and illustrated the concerns and worries of all participants in the process. The need for confidential counselling seemed to be demonstrated.

The Scottish Council for Single Parents, in providing an adoptive information service for statutory and voluntary agencies in Scotland, regards its service as a means of helping applicants to avoid a lengthy search for information about available children. The Council despatches to agencies information, gathered three times a year, showing whether and where lists are open for the placing of young babies, older children, physically or mentally handicapped children and children of mixed racial origin. Agencies can thus quickly direct inquirers to an appropriate agency.

It was not only adoptive home finding for hard-to-place or special need children that concerned agencies with regard to future developments. The question of adoption for siblings was also important. York Adoption Society, which had always encouraged adopters to take two children found that, in a sample of their placements over the period 1968 to 1974, 128 children had been adopted by 80 couples and 74 per cent of the children had a brother or sister placed by the society. These were mainly children placed under the age of one year. A future problem, recognised by agencies in general was the placement of or separation of older siblings if a permanent adoptive home were to be found.

Three examples of innovations by voluntary agencies follow.

Durham Diocesan Family Welfare Council

Although the Council provides fostering services, it has developed and is expanding towards a comprehensive adoption agency for Gateshead, South Tyneside, Sunderland, Durham and Cleveland (North of the Tees). It is aiming to coordinate data from local agencies to develop a more effective referral source and is working towards a multi-denominational service with appropriate representation at committee level from other Churches and from the participant local authorities.

A Handbook for Catholic Agencies

The Catholic Child Welfare Council established a Working Party to consider the implications of the Children Act, 1975, particularly with regard to registration. After visiting all 17 Catholic Diocesan Agencies concerned with adoption, the Council published a handbook which discussed criteria, standards, procedures and general principles.

The principles adopted stress contact with the putative father and his right to be heard on matters concerning the future of the child, the older child's need to be aware of his biography, preferably in visible form, and the requirement to inform all the parties of the right of access to records at the age of 18. It was decided to retain a lay committee because it provided a neutral panel to protect the interests of parents, children and adopters and to support social workers.

Adoption Parties

These parties are a new development which are arousing interest as a future initiative capable of many variations. Parent-to-Parent Information on Adoption Services, with the co-operation of the Adoption Resource Exchange and several London Boroughs and voluntary agencies, have set up a small experimental project 'adoption parties' as a way of finding adoptive parents for hard-to-place children, older children, handicapped children and black children. These parties provide a relatively safe and neutral meeting ground for would-be adoptive parents and children who need permanent homes. Some of the children are not legally free for adoption but legal adoption may be possible at a later date.

Four parties have been held; two on Saturdays in 1976 and two on Saturdays in 1977. About two months before a party, there is a meeting when adoption officers bring details of children they would like to include. The number and age range of the children and the number of couples to be invited are discussed. About two weeks before the party, the couples are invited to a planning meeting together with the children's social workers and residential workers. The couples are told about the children who will be coming and then organise the party, the games, entertainment and food.

At one party there were 12 children aged between five and 12 mostly of mixed race (some were siblings) and ten couples. One party was exclusively for black and mixed race children. There were 17 children and ten couples including four West Indian families and two mixed-marriage couples. The fourth party was for older children aged ten to 15 years and took the form of a barbeque supper.

At the end of each party the couples were given a list of the children, with a brief profile of each child and his family situation, and the name and telephone number of the child's social worker who planned to be available in the area office on the following Monday morning.

A discussion evening is held about ten days after each party when social workers, adoption officers, couples and organisers can talk over their feelings and, if possible, hear of any comments made by the children; and couples and social workers can express their concerns and anxieties. These meetings have enabled PPIAS to evaluate the results and problems of this means of home finding. They conclude that the parties are a viable method of finding new families for certain children particularly since they bring in the element of self-selection. A number of children have been placed as a result of these parties.

Fostering

More than 20 local authorities and the major voluntary organizations were considering initiatives, other than schemes for adolescents, in fostering programmes to meet differing sets of circumstances requiring mainly short-stay help. A group of these agencies planned what one authority termed 'respite care'. Short-stay foster homes are planned for handicapped children who normally live at home, in hospital, in residential care or occasionally in long-stay foster homes. Respite care is not limited to fostering pre-arranged through the agency. It includes the possibilities of direct contact between the natural family and a foster family recognised by the agency as experienced and skilled. The aim is to enable the natural family and child to have the security of a known alternative in an emergency, during a holiday or for an occasional break.

There are a few experiments in hand, or being planned, to use foster homes for remand, interim care order or assessment purposes and as part of an Intermediate Treatment programme. In some cases, they are to be outposts of assessment centres where the professional services are concentrated. In other instances, the foster family and community services provide the assessment. Similar proposals include short term therapeutic fostering to relieve tension in a crisis of acting out behaviour.

A small group of agencies are concerned about methods of giving individual care and treatment to kinship related children without splitting them up as a family. Foster homes specially recruited and supported to provide family care for several children and a planned package of domiciliary services to maintain the children in their own homes or variants of group foster homes are among the proposals. Five agencies are interested in providing or subsidising the rent or mortgage payments of houses large enough to enable experienced foster parents to care for a family of children. Some agencies have access to property; others propose to subsidise a large foster home in the family's accommodation. Lodgings, rather than foster homes, are seen as practical for young people over the age of sixteen, for single pregnant girls, and for young mothers with their babies. Many of these ideas reflected very local needs or the response of a group of social workers confronted with a lack of alternative resources or a strong belief in the value of family placement.

Organizational developments

About 20 authorities aim to increase the sophistication of their child and family services. They contemplate organizational changes to accommodate development projects, to produce procedural guidance, to manage publicity and recruitment and to implement policy changes in general or special schemes in particular. Family placement schemes are attractive for professional, ideological or economic reasons. Where policies are proposed, it has not always been decided how to implement them. Their objectives include a first or further review of children in care as a baseline for policy decisions, the formal adoption of a family placement policy or the management of an organized attempt to develop combined preventive and care services for families and children.

Policy Statements

Clarification of policy issues for the development of standardised procedures are seen as an important future task. Policy statements have been issued by about one-fifth of the respondent agencies, but in some cases the statements are not available for reasons of confidentiality. They are generally the result of working parties of officers. They set out aims and objectives and the methods for achieving them. The headings of some statements give an idea of the variety – 'Guidelines on assessment of situations involving children', 'Model of decision making for children', 'An adoption counselling service', 'Proposals for the development of foster care', 'Support to foster parents', 'Guidelines on the assessment of substitute homes', 'Adoption as part of a comprehensive service for children'.

Procedural Manuals

About one-fifth of all statutory agencies have issued procedural manuals for their staff but more frequently for fostering than for adoption. The production of manuals figures very highly among the initiatives to be taken when resources allow. There is clearly felt to be a need for them. When they do come to be written, some choices about the type of manual will need to be made. Existing manuals vary from a rule book, through codified professional practice, to guidelines which set out general principles. Most of them are internal documents but East Sussex has published a 'Guide to Practice'. The interest in the potentiality of such manuals raises questions about their purposes:

Is a rule book manual a bureaucratic safety device to protect the agency or is it an essential tool for practitioners and administrators?

Is a rule book likely to generate conflict because it requires too much attention to administrative detail and to operational checks?

Is codified professional practice a valuable unifying exercise for administrators and professionals?

Is codification necessary for standardising the basic procedures common to generic and specialised practice?

Is general guidance adequate without ready access to specialist advice?

Is it more helpful to combine or to separate practice guidelines and systems procedures?

Voluntary agencies, being not only smaller in size and specialised in task, have had less need to codify their procedures and can more frequently settle them through Resource Exchanges. Nevertheless, they were faced with having to analyse and make their arrangements explicit.

Consultation in Policy Making

Developments in fostering were referred to far more frequently than those in adoption practice. This is partly because family placement for fostering and adoption is increasingly seen as embodying similar processes, skills and standards and partly because foster placements far out number adoptive placements.

The most frequent comments relate to attitudinal changes. A significant number of statutory agencies indicated that their attitudes were changing towards consultation with foster parents. Both ABAFA and NFCA have clearly been influential and instrumental in providing national and local forums for consideration of policy and practice developments.

There was evidence that statutory agencies are actively seeking to involve foster parents in consultation on planning and policy appropriate to the locality. In other cases, direct approaches from foster parents to the agency are meeting with a positive response. Consultation was nearly always referred to as of recent origin but over 30 statutory agencies had already found some means of effecting it and intended further development.

The readiest means of consultation is with the local foster care associations which are affiliated to NFCA and are being helped to take up a consultative role. At one extreme, the consultation with the local foster care association is at elected member level on a regular basis. At the other extreme, social workers are themselves attempting to form groups of foster parents. In between, there are foster parents who meet regularly in groups but prefer not to affiliate to NFCA. This independence does not necessarily prevent them from welcoming consultation. By no means all foster parents wish to be involved in policy and planning; many prefer to convey their individual reactions to the social worker.

Consultation processes, even when regarded as part of the policy of the local authority, are not always evenly developed geographically. Where there is considerable area autonomy, there is more enthusiasm in some areas than in others or more pressure from foster parents. It seems clear that, whatever the pattern developed for consultation and however formal or informal it is, there is an overall development towards recognising its value. Weather, distance, and travelling problems were all mentioned as obstacles to regular consultation, particularly in rural areas and in the winter, but these factors were usually mentioned as obstacles to be overcome rather than as negative indicators.

The areas of consultation most frequently mentioned are financial arrangements, administrative procedures, new initiatives, publicity, recruitment, training and exchange of ideas. A few agencies see training as a means of consultation. Seminar and discussion groups automatically produce reactions to current policy and practice but the more marked tendency is to make a distinction between consultation on policy and feedback from training.

At least two local authorities, Devon and Durham, have included representative foster parents on policy development working parties and two others, Bexley and Tayside, are working with foster parents to produce a practical handbook for the joint use of foster parents and staff.

Neither formal nor informal consultation between agencies and foster parents seems to have raised major issues at this stage though administrative arrangements for payments are a serious problem. The major issue for the future may well be less about the desirability of consultation as such, but rather more about the balance of power as between the agency, the social workers and the foster parents.

There are some other issues which concern consultation on planning and policy:

Is planning for family placement for children likely to become a more democratic process for this client group than for other client groups and, if so, how is the balance of interests to be maintained? It should be noted that the difference is that children are legally in a dependency status whereas other client groups may be dependent in all material circumstances but are in most cases deemed capable of decision making.

How are the interests of all parties to family placement to be represented in policy formation if only foster parents and social workers are articulate? In comparison, children and natural parents may be relatively powerless and inarticulate.

How is an agency to develop a consultation process with all foster parents as distinct from those who belong to a particular organization?

Community alternatives

Just under twenty agencies were concerned to invest in alternatives designed to avoid the separation of child and natural family. These agencies saw day fostering, informal emergency arrangements, homehelps, childminders and children's centres as promising developments in community care offering support to families. This objective came closest to the 'unitary approach', now so popular in North America (Specht and Vickery, 1977) as a means of assessing local needs and developing local strategies to match needs and resources. An example of an alternative scheme is quoted.

Lothian Selected Landladies Scheme for Young People

This is a proposed joint project between Area 5 in Lothian and the Council of West End Churches to provide accommodation for 3 or 4 young women in the age range 16 to 19 years who are ready to leave, or have left a children's home or hostel.

The Council of West End Churches is buying a property and allowing it to be used for the project. The Council will provide up to £20,000 to cover the purchase of a flat, furnishing and repairs and ongoing maintenance. The rent will be fixed within the limits laid down for the scheme and will include fuel costs. The rent will be met by the young people but the social work department will guarantee its payment. The flat will provide one room for each girl plus a communal room, a kitchen and a bathroom.

There will be liaison and co-operation between the Council of West End Churches and the staff of Area 5. Field social work and residential staff will be involved in the preparatory stages of placement and in subsequent support. The project, initially for one year, is to be reviewed at the end of that period on the assumption that the property is a resource which can be used to meet other community needs if this scheme proves to be a disappointment.

Resource Exchanges

A small group of agencies foresaw that an active family placement policy for children with special needs was likely to be best achieved through their involvement in inter-agency exchange of resources rather than exclusively within their own organization. They deliberately sought future development through these exchanges.

The growth of resource exchanges and inter-agency co-operation outside any formal statutory machinery was the major area of interaction between statutory and voluntary agencies. This development may be seen as a preparation for the comprehensive adoption service proposed in the Children Act, 1975. These informal arrangements may be a way of neutralising the status and power rivalries of statutory and voluntary agencies. Voluntary agencies have, in some cases, taken the lead and contributed funding for inter-agency co-operation. The current inquiry did not specifically ask for information about Resource Exchanges but so many statutory and voluntary agencies referred to them that detailed information was sought. Examples of various resource exchanges for family placement are given here not only because of their intrinsic interest but because they may well be a pointer to future co-operation and shared development between statutory and voluntary agencies.

Adoption Resource Exchange (ARE)

Home finding for non-white babies was the original concern of the Adoption Resource Exchange which was first proposed in 1968 and, through the co-operative efforts of a few statutory and voluntary agencies, succeeded in providing a linkage system which enabled nine babies to be placed during the first year. Since then ARE has been instrumental in assisting member agencies to place some 800 children. This group of children includes not only mixed race babies but children up to the age of 12, those who have a physical or mental handicap or severe medical problems and those who need a family where they can remain together as brothers and sisters.

ARE exists to provide a national exchange service to enable member agencies to cooperate in the exchange of children and adoptive families. The view is that the adoption of hard-to-place children in this country still requires a profound change in attitude, objective and conduct within the population at large and within some professional circles. In this climate, ARE maintains regular and aggressive publicity. ARE handled the unexpectedly high response to Granada's television programme 'World in Action' in 1974. (Details of this response are given in *Table 7*). It has supported 'Reports Action' since this programme, which was originally for the North West of England, became a national programme. ARE was also involved in the 'Soul Kids' campaign mounted by a group of London statutory and voluntary agencies in an attempt to find 'black families' for 'black' children. ARE is concerned to ensure that active publicity contains a social work input as well as maximum protection for any children actually taking part. For advice on their home finding features, Granada TV has a social work group composed of social workers nominated by ARE.

In contrast to aggressive propaganda seeking family experience for hard-to-place children, professional practice within the link-up service relies on peaceful penetration. The belief is that in the matching of children and families, exploitation of either would be unethical.

In the interests of setting and maintaining professional standards, membership of ARE is by invitation. Membership implies that the agency fulfills agreed criteria regarding adequacy of service. It also involves members in a moral commitment to opening up adoption opportunities by finding and sharing children and families to create a national pool of resources. To secure the basis of trust in using the services of another agency, ARE reviews its membership every two years by means of a questionnaire and a review meeting with all levels of staff within a member agency. This evaluation leads to a statement of current practice and then adherence to agreed criteria until the next review of the member agency. Within the agreed criteria, members then follow their own particular practice with regard to placement. Some place direct for adoption but although about 60 per cent of the placements start as fostering, adoption is the clear goal of ARE.

ARE became an independent charitable organisation in 1975 relying on grants from government, from trusts and on the current fee of £150 chargeable to each member agency which makes a placement through ARE resources. Any member agency is investing in an ethical bank account in that it undertakes to share families as well as children. In practice, however, many local authorities in membership tend to see their membership as an investment for finding families to adopt the hard-to-place children in their care. It is a fact that 65 per cent of the adoptive families have been recruited through voluntary agency members in the last financial year. But without the finding and sharing of families, ARE cannot operate. This principle is inviolate whether resource exchange systems are operated nationally, regionally or within a large agency.

South-East Scotland Resource Centre

The South-East Scotland Resource Centre developed from informal discussions between statutory and voluntary agencies about the desirability of greater co-operation between agencies to provide a more co-ordinated service both for single parents and for the placement of children in permanent substitute families. An advisory Committee for Inter-Agency Co-operation was formed; the Resource Centre has been its major project to date and the one which required funding to employ an organiser and secretary. Finance for an experimental three-year period was obtained from the Scottish Social Work Services Group and now that the service is established, the Centre is supported by grants from the member local authorities.

The initial grant, by agreement, was channelled through the Guild of Service, Edinburgh, the agency which continues to provide a base for the service. The objective is similar to that of ARE. Information is obtained about children identified as needing permanent placement and about families offering such homes and links are suggested. As the main needs are for homes for school-age children, sibling groups and handicapped children, it has been agreed that efforts should be made to develop local potential. Membership is open to all local authorities in S.E. Scotland together with voluntary agencies concerned with child placement.

In 1974, the first year of operation, six children were placed through the Resource Centre. By 1977 this number had risen to 92. Approximately three-quarters of the families were provided by voluntary agencies who are increasingly linking their work to the needs identified by the local authorities responsible for the children. The growth of interest in the placement of children with special needs is very evident within the local authorities; during 1977 as many as 12 children were withdrawn from referral to the Centre because their referring agency had subsequently found a suitable placement.

To facilitate the development of trust among agencies, referral procedures were carefully established. As agency cooperation has grown, there has been an increasing wish for joint discussion of practice and procedures and a strong interest in sharing experience and developing expertise. A network of 'contact members' within agencies has been established to facilitate communication and to be available to support workers who may be involved in an inter-agency placement. The Centre itself may also act as a 'neutral ground' when difficulties arise between agencies.

Other roles for the Resource Centre are the provision of general information about both needs and practice in that statistics and a newsbulletin are produced. The Exchange offers a forum to consider an inter-agency approach to such aspects as recruitment, publicity, and new methods which include adoption parties. Future developments may include increasing links with other areas of Scotland and also more clearly defined links with ARE.

South Wales Working Party

All local authorities and most voluntary agencies in South Wales have formed a Working Party on Fostering and Adoption. This is currently collecting case material on 'Introductions of children into long term homes' as a means of illustrating good practice and procedure for member agencies.

London & Regional Fostering Group

This group of fostering officers from 33 London Boroughs, from six major national voluntary organisations, and from some South East Counties started in 1974 with the aim of promoting fostering developments in London. The total group now operates through five geographical sub-groups to share problems and resources and break down territorial possessiveness. Its major achievement so far has been in publicity aimed at raising the public awareness of the needs of children in care.The total group mounted the 'Mums and Dads' campaign in 1976 as a promotional exercise for home finding for black children in London and the South East. Under the umbrella of the campaign, with its TV, radio and press coverage, participating authorities retained freedom to respond to inquirers according to their individual arrangements and freedom to mount their own recruitment efforts as a follow-up to general publicity.

It was the London Fostering Group which undertook to provide children and case histories for the media publicity. As a federation of London Boroughs and neighbouring counties, its task so far has been mainly in public relations rather than in the exchange of resources but its major impact has been to exert group pressure on individual authorities to develop thinking, practice, training and a new attitude towards the sharing of skills, ideas, initiatives, publicity and child and family placements. It is a voluntary federation manned by agency fostering officers without any formal bureaucratic support.

North Regional Children's Resource Service

The North Regional Group of Adoption and Fostering Agencies, comprising nine local authorities and five voluntary bodies located within the area covered by the North Regional Children's Planning Committee, formed a Resource Service in November, 1976. A member agency, the Church of England Children's Society, undertook wholly to finance the service for the first three years after which an alternative source of funds is to be sought. The service has no other independent income of its own except that each member agency pays an annual sum of £10. When a child in the care of one of the member local authorities is legally adopted by a family found by one of the member voluntary agencies, then that agency receives a fee of two hundred and fifty pounds from the local authority concerned.

The Resource is a referral service for linking hard-to-place children and adoptive and foster families. It seeks to provide a comprehensive regional service with standardised procedures for inter-agency cooperation and a sharing of resources. As a promotional body it hopes to assist two member agencies, one statutory and one voluntary, to mount a recruitment campaign for fostering and adoptive homes. Negotiations are continuing with the Manpower Services Commission for this project to be acceptable to the job creation scheme and, in that event, a research assistant would be employed to use community work methods to raise the level of public awareness of the needs of children in care. This is an example of the way in which the resource service hopes to identify locally available resources and coordinate their use.

Although this resource service aims to promote high standards, its membership is geographical. Agencies are not required to fulfill certain criteria before being admitted to membership. Membership involves a commitment to sharing information, experiences and resources.

Other inter-agency transactions

Twelve Children's Regional Planning Committees were established in England and Wales under the Children and Young Persons Act, 1969, to plan residential provision for children. Although there has been no statutory bar to using this machinery for planning and consulting over other aspects of children's services, the machinery has in the main been side stepped and other less formal arrangements have been preferred for developing inter-agency family placement transactions. The fact that voluntary agencies are not in membership of Children's Regional Planning Committees may have contributed to the development of separate forms of association to promote family placement.

As an example, the Church of England Children's Society has deployed a senior social worker in Bristol to act as a co-ordinator for the Children's Resource Service which has produced a code of practice. The code, subsequently endorsed by the Children's Regional Planning Committee, covers assessment of children's needs, work with natural families, foster and adoption applicants, placement procedure and support service.

An even less formalised arrangement is the Merseyside Adoption and Fostering Consortium. This consists of one local voluntary adoption agency, four national children's agencies represented at area level and five local authorities. The agencies of the consortium aim to give advice to parents and to women and girls on pregnancy as well as on adoption and fostering. Its most recent concerted activity has been to link up with NFCA to organize, through the media, a campaign to recruit foster parents for children aged over seven years.

The Council for Christian Care (Devon) offers an illustration of voluntary agency initiative in facilitating inter-agency transactions.

Devon Council for Christian Care

In 1974 the former Devon Diocesan Council for Family and Social Welfare, anticipating the passing of the Children Act, 1975, called together all the voluntary adoption agencies in the South West to consider the Houghton Committee's recommendations (HMSO 1972). A formal approach was then made to all the local authority social service departments within the South West Children's Regional Planning area. After two and a half years of consultation, the Children's Planning Committee was itself involved, and, in July 1977, it endorsed the creation of the South West

Regional Children's Resource Service.

A code of practice has been agreed by all the participating agencies and a management committee has been established. The Resource Service provides for close co-operation between local authority and voluntary agencies in finding foster or adoptive homes for the more difficult and hard-to-place children. The Church of England Children's Society has agreed to make available, for a three-year-period, the services of a senior social worker based in Bristol for three days a week to act as co-ordinator for the exchange of homes and children. The co-ordinator attempts to suggest suitable placements and then puts the responsible social workers in touch with one another.

The Council have discussed their future adoption policy with the Devon social services department and have appointed an adoption officer to be responsible for their adoption work and to represent them on the Children's Resource Service. The cost of this appointment is to be met by a grant from the Devon social services department.

Chapter 9
Some practice developments

Selection in homefinding

Two trends were noticeable in the process of homefinding. Firstly, an individual or casework selection process was being developed within a set of guidelines and, secondly, group work was becoming part of the selection process.

The casework approach

The process involves the family and, later, relatives or significant friends and helpers in a two way selection process which allows the family and agency to withdraw without acute feelings of resentment and rejection. With this framework initial discussions provide opportunities for exchange of information between the family and the agency and for exploration on a 'no obligation' basis. Once the exploratory stage is completed, the formal application is introduced and signifies some commitment on either side to justify the pursuit of the health and character inquiries. The next phase, if reached, tends to be more concerned with some acknowledged commitment which warrants a further exploration of motivation, feelings, attitudes, ways of managing past and present relationships within the marriage, the family and the neighbourhood. In the management of this phased approach some of the principles of *Foster Care — a Guide to Practice* (HMSO, 1976) have been influential. Some agencies have established guidelines for exploring attitudes and reactions to normal and abnormal child behaviour, for assessing emotional resilience and ability to use friendship and community resources.

From the stage of the completed application, detailed procedural checks begin to operate and specialist fostering and/or adoption officers may be involved. Where these exist, they may be used as additional assessors or, if the placement is not being prepared for a particular child, they may accept the home as an agency rather than an area team resource and maintain contact through visits to the family until a placement is made.

The casework and group work approaches should not be seen as other than complementary; the variation lies in the emphasis given to each by different agencies or area teams. This description and the group work description which follows are archetypes derived from handbooks and procedures developed by fostering and adoption units or by working parties.

The group work approach

More than twenty statutory agencies and many voluntary agencies saw group work as the practice area they wished to develop at all stages of family placement. Shortage of experienced group workers and of education and training facilities were seen as impediments.

A group work approach to selection is aimed at enabling families to select themselves for fostering or adoption, or, as illustrated in some of the projects, is the precursor to further involvement in groups for specific preparation, training, placement and support. This continuing group work process was a more common feature in projects specially designed for home finding for hard-to-place children. But where group work had to be rationed, it was typically used at the initial information and early selection stages both in the statutory and voluntary sectors.

The first approach to an agency might be met with the offer of a choice between a home or office interview or an invitation to a group meeting. In some cases, when there is a firm commitment to group work, only the latter is offered with the promise of a home interview at a later stage. Agencies which had decided on a particular pattern often expressed anxiety about first encounters. Were individual interviews or group meetings more effective? They stressed the need to learn more about the loss of interest and drop-out rate at this initial stage. Lack of time often prevented a follow up visit when a couple dropped out, but there were many suggestions that this was an area requiring closer scrutiny before any conclusions could be drawn about effective first encounters. One suggestion was that first encounters should be with an experienced foster or adoptive parent rather than with the agency.

There was much more consensus about the purpose of initial group meetings; they are for information exchange. They require the agency to share accurate information about its objectives and needs. The next phase concerns a more detailed study of the children, their current placement, their natural family and social relationships and their anticipated responses to the pressures of life with a new family. Experienced foster and adoptive parents and residential social workers may be involved at this stage. While there was great variation in the timing of the home visit and the completion of the application forms, it seemed that frankness about the personal investigation procedures was regarded as vital.

The group work model meets with obvious practical difficulties. Agencies mentioned the shortage of social workers who felt comfortable in meeting with groups; there were travel and accommodation problems in rural areas: the timing of the groups often conflicted with the employment commitments of applicants whose children also had to be catered for.

All of these factors complicated the logistics of a group selection process when compared with prearranged individual home or office visits. Advocates of the group work approach favourably contrasted it with the more traditional investigatory, vetting, approval and rejection procedure associated with earlier practice dominated by a rigid regulatory approach but those who preferred the casework approach made similar claims for it.

This superficial description of the casework and group approach to selection suggests that attitudinal changes rather than dogma are influencing practice in both models. Vocabulary associated with an investigatory and authoritarian procedure is giving way to terms which reflect mutual selection and decision making. For example, families tended to be 'accepted' and 'accepting' rather than 'vetted' and 'approved' or 'rejected'. Home finding, family placement and fostering are becoming preferred terms to 'boarding out' and 'children's services' are replacing the term 'child care' which, in its historical context has excluded day and domiciliary support services.

Involvement in decision making and planning

It naturally followed that agencies which opened up their planning to the comments and reactions of foster or adoption parents tended to involve them in more detailed decision making and planning for individual children. It was at this level of shared decision-making that local voluntary agencies, in particular, commented positively on their experience of continued involvement with short-term foster parents and with adopters especially with those who adopted more than one child. This type of interaction tended to be an intimate and continuing relationship because there was often a shared denominational religious affiliation which helped to develop loyalty and support for the agency, and regular efforts were made to engage families in fund raising, recruitment, and various agency tasks. This type of relationship was a voluntary service link between the families and the agency rather than a deliberate attempt to involve the families in decision-making with professional agency staff. A similar agency loyalty and informal group support system, was clearly developing in some places between local authority area teams or groups of specialist officers and local foster care associations.

The most frequent area of involvement was in relation to reviews of children either regularly or on an *ad hoc* basis. A few statutory agencies preferred the review to take place in the foster home making use of the child's knowledge and/or presence and expecting a written record to be prepared by the foster parents. Rather more agencies included foster parents, children and natural parents, when possible, in reviews. The preparation and sharing of illustrated biographies and scrap books was also referred to as a valuable tool, especially in residential social work and for review purposes. It was an important record for the child and the families. This was a task which involved communication among all those who had

had some relationship with the child and might include staff from several services.

Consultation with children

Some twenty agencies commented upon their attempts to involve older children in decisions about plans for their future. Children's groups, as such, did not figure largely and attendance was voluntary. Individual preparatory work with social workers seemed more frequent though it proved difficult to make any realistic estimate of the extent of consultation with children whether in individual or group meetings. Practice varied within agencies or had been developed more with children in residential care or more with foster children rather than as a universal pattern common to all older children. Certainly consultation was more developed with children being considered for long stay placement than for short stay placement.

Support for waiting foster parents and adopters

The characteristic reply to the request for information under this heading indicated a growing awareness of the importance of support and its vital significance at the pre-placement stage. It was recognised that potential foster parents could be lost during the waiting period when they were keyed up to receive a child. They and their relatives could be puzzled and frustrated by constant recruitment publicity while they continued to wait for a child and lacked both attention and explanation. To avoid such a situation, several agencies had recently introduced, or were in the process of starting, a service for waiting families. The service varied from occasional postal communication, the despatch of a regular newsletter, involvement in sporadic meetings or social gatherings to the provision of a programme of preparation.

Another means of support came through participation in the activities of local foster care associations. A few agencies relied almost completely on local associations to provide support.

There was both awareness and anxiety about support for adopters waiting for very young babies. With lists either closed, or open only for limited periods, and with waiting periods known to extend up to two years, the provision of useful support during this indefinite period posed considerable problems. This situation was too unpredictable for other than occasional visiting, the provision of regular information and, more rarely, some group experience. It was during this rather unstructured contact that some families learned about the needs of hard-to-place children.

Education and training

Nearly twenty statutory and most of the voluntary organizations, put a high priority on extending education and training opportunities for all participants in family placement. Lack of time, of expertise, of agreement on content or personnel and concern about actual training facilities were noted as obstacles to be overcome when diversified family placement was adopted as a future policy. So far, the most significant developments involved formalised in-service training, the practice of group work and the move towards involving foster parents, adopters and residential and field social workers in joint learning situations.

The types of in-service education and training are of great variety, and the influence and practical help of ABAFA is obvious. Nearly all active agencies have developed some form of in-service training and nearly half of all statutory agencies have devised comprehensive programmes relating to family placement in general but with greater emphasis on fostering. Adoption continues to remain somewhat separate and training needs to be short-term, intensive and legalistic.

In general terms, broadly based in-service training for family placement, although it has often started by being restricted to brief induction and orientation day sessions, has begun to move into longer residential phases and to become more complex. Some agencies with specialized officers or fostering and adoption units use them to provide many levels of educational training for social workers, foster parents, adopters and involve them all in teaching as well as in learning. In creating these internal training programmes, training sections sometimes play a prominent part but less so, it seems, as the number of specialized fostering and adoption officers increases.

Some training is highly formalised and based on a course of lectures given by internal and external experts on various subjects which nearly always include law, agency administration and practice, community services, child development and relationships with natural parents. Those responsible for such programmes stress that, although the presentation may appear formal, there is a generous allowance of time for discussion at every session. Programmes of this kind have a close resemblance to evening class sessions. In general, there is little reference to the use of films or video tape material and the time allocated to the study of child development seems limited.

Local authorities which rely on colleges are widely scattered geographically except for a group of London Boroughs sharing a joint programme mounted by one college for all of them. College based courses tend to be formally structured, though it is emphasised that time is available for discussion and, again, there is little reference to film or video tape material. Some of these courses are open to foster parents and, in a few cases, the agency pays the foster parents' fees.

In some areas, training, whatever form it takes, cuts across some traditional boundaries particularly when groups are the target of training. The variety of patterns for groups is considerable and it is difficult to distinguish between those used mainly for support and those used explicitly for training. Barnsley has arranged a weekly club to support foster parents and childminders with an accompanying creche and toy library; another agency holds a weekly group for short-stay foster parents and a third agency provides by way of contrast, a fifteen session group work course of a very demanding nature.

Issues about training for family placement relate to its purpose, extent and provenance.

How far is training specific to individual agency practice?

Should joint training sessions be provided for families and newly recruited agency staff?

How far can scarce training resources be shared between statutory and voluntary agencies?

Should training be based and provided within the agency or within an educational establishment?

What are the appropriate boundaries for training?

Should training relate only to fostering and adoption or is it appropriate to include those involved in other services for children such as residential care, playgroups, daily minding or day fostering?

There remains the issue of the practice of excellence. If the quality of family placement is to be developed to a high level, dissipation of training resources may not be appropriate in the future. It may be necessary to ask whether, at least in the short-term, training for different tasks and types of placements should be made available in a few centres so as to attract the most skilled teachers and experts in order to disseminate the best practice. It may also be necessary to ask whether film and video tape should make a more significant contribution to adult learning and whether family therapy, behaviour modification, psychodrama and other approaches and processes should be included in this learning. Those agencies which wish to invest resources in training for family placement in the future may well need to decide between being self contained or attached to a centre of excellence.

Chapter 10
The current situation

The Children Act, 1975

At the time of this inquiry, the impact of this legislation seemed to be confined largely to attitudinal changes, to giving out information about the legislative position and to a consideration of the respective roles of statutory and voluntary agencies. As already indicated liaison between statutory and voluntary adoption agencies has increased mainly through the development of Resource Exchanges rather than through formal arrangements (page 88). A few statutory authorities had either recently become or were intending to become adoption agencies and attributed this decision to the passing of the Act. A small group of statutory authorities had made formal arrangements for local voluntary adoption agencies to undertake particular adoption functions; conversely, some local voluntary agencies had made a deliberate decision to restrict their geographical coverage in order to work more closely with a particular statutory authority. Many agencies indicated that they were making more active use of material supplied by ABAFA, so that some procedural uniformity was developing. This seemed to be a preparatory period for working towards the full implementation of the Act rather than one of conscious activity occasioned by a new piece of legislation on the statute book. The situation still remained that, in a few parts of the country, presumably because of resource restraints, neither the statutory authority acted as an adoption agency nor was there a local voluntary adoption agency. Prospective adopters had to rely upon national agencies and the passing of the legislation had not, so far, altered this situation by creating a local and accessible service.

The Children Act, 1975, was one of several factors which has led to a recent increased interest in family placement, paradoxically, at a time of increased concern over violence within the family, non-accidental injury to children and diversification of family life styles. Agencies tended to see developments occurring as a result of a combination of influences described earlier (page 16) rather than the single and direct result of the legislation itself. There was frequent reference to the means chosen to disseminate information about the legislative provisions so far enacted. Many agencies had made use of leaflets or handbooks to spell out, for example, the new grounds for assumption of parental rights. A few specifically commented that these extended grounds had proved to be helpful and that significantly more resolutions had been passed. But there were indications that the need to consider whether a resolution was required had been built into reviews. There was no indication that there had been other than a cautious approach to the use of this extended power.

It did not appear that the requirement to give one month's notice before removing a child from care after a period of six months' stay had caused dramatic changes. Explanations, given in leaflets or handbooks, tended to be factual and to point out the advantages of preparing a child for a move. Only one statutory authority made a positive comment that this requirement was of advantage in preventing precipitate discharge.

One marked indirect effect of the Children Act, 1975, was to increase the recognition of the complexities of the legislation affecting children and to increase communication between agencies and families. Information about legislative provisions featured prominently in all types of training programmes. Training was having to carry an increased legalistic burden. One agency had delegated the task of information giving about the new legislation to the local foster care association but, in general, agencies regarded it as a new responsibility placed on them by the Act to ensure that foster parents and others involved in family placement were basically equipped to understand their legal rights. Durham stressed the need to give verbal as well as written explanations of the legislation. Experience showed that some foster parents seemed apparently to be under the impression that they were obliged, or expected, to apply for the adoption of a child they had fostered for over five years.

In terms of attitudinal change, about twenty agencies indicated that it was the Children Act, 1975, which had caused them to set up working parties to review the needs of their population of children in care and to work out strategies for long-stay children. Another group of about twenty agencies perceived the new legislation as having been instrumental in causing the options of fostering and adoption to be considered at reviews of children.

One of the far reaching provisions of the Children Act, 1975, was the right given to adopted adults (at least 18 years old) to have access, if they wish, to their original birth records. This right fundamentally alters the character of adoption which can no longer be regarded necessarily as the complete and permanent severance of ties between the adoptee and the natural parents or siblings. This is, however, only a new right in England and Wales (DHSS, 1976); Scottish law has previously permitted this access. Although there was plenty of evidence that steps were being taken to inform all parties to adoption orders of the existence of this new right in England and Wales, there was as yet little indication of any dramatic reactions to this change. Comments on the response to requests for counselling before an adopted adult sought access to birth records was, at this early stage, confined to three main reactions:

1. the recognition of the importance of detailed record-keeping. One agency had noted that eight people over the age of thirty had made an ap-

proach in order to acquire a birth certificate and several agencies referred
to the importance to be attached to the safe custody and transfer of birth
certificates and other personal documentation;
2. the increase, apparently a small one and referred to by only a few
agencies, in the actual counsellings of adopted adults;
3. the allocation of responsibility for counselling to an experienced and
senior practitioner.

The new legislation was noted in connection with three research studies.
One, mounted jointly by Gloucestershire and ABAFA, was a study of
adoption counselling. Devon hoped to discover what a counselling service
brought to light about adoption experiences and Birmingham social services department and the University of Surrey were each beginning studies
of the attitudes of adopters and foster parents to the provisions of the 1975
Act.

The organizational problem

This inquiry indicated that there was anxiety about generic and specialized
areas of work, about the conflict between a unit set up to promote development in family placement or a special scheme and about hierarchical
responsibilities. Suffice it to say that long term family placement and short
term treatment of very complex children may require highly specialized
knowledge, a period of model-building for practice and research purposes
and close working arrangements with other professional disciplines. The
important question to ask may be whether innovatory work requires a
period of concentration and specialization in relation to the development
of a particular service for any client group.

There is a further problem, in this sphere, in that the statutory agencies
are concerned with many client groups for which they provide common services: the voluntary agencies, whether for fostering or adoption or for
both, give a specialized service to particular client groups. Whether voluntary agencies decide to specialize further or to diversify, they continue to
need to be able to relate to identifiable people in a large organization if co-
operative activity is to be pursued.

Further, voluntary agencies may decide to provide choices and alternatives and to innovate. But statutory agencies clearly wished to innovate
too. One of the issues is how to facilitate development in large scale
organizations and enable experiments to survive.

Attitudes towards family placement

Finally, a set of key issues are attitudinal in character. There was no
evidence, from this inquiry, that political ideologies affected family placement policy and practice. When there was elected member backing, it gave
thrust to policy and priority for it. Sectarian influence, though present in
the voluntary sector, did not appear over pronounced. Some voluntary
agencies continued, quite properly, to respect a mandate, usually inherent

in their foundation, to work with families and children of a particular religious denomination. Others, while continuing to fulfil this mandate, were extending the boundaries of their work and their clientele. Professional influence was strong when it was organized and mobilized to propose policy options and achieve commitment from management, from social work colleagues and local communities.

Family placement neither appeared to be, nor is it likely to be, free from conflict. It is concerned with legal and assumed rights which are claimed when emotion or obligation creates or destroys loyalties. Family placement is concerned with the transfer of power and requires opportunities for the development and expression of feelings. Perhaps the basic questions that family placement seeks to answer in special ways are 'where does the child in care put his feelings?', 'where do the adults concerned put theirs?' The strength of these feelings, and the respect due to them, in good professional practice, was emphasised in *Foster Care: A Guide to Practice* (HMSO, 1976). More pronounced conflict can be anticipated in the changing attitude towards adoption as a means of giving older or institutionalized children, who may retain family memories and ties, the security of permanence in a family setting during childhood.

Family placement is unlikely to escape society's current concern and confusion about the institution of the family as a social system and a cultural unit for the transmission of norms and values (Rapoport, 1977). Whether the family is disintegrating or becoming flexible enough to accommodate many life styles is sufficiently debatable to cause attitudes to become complex in relation to natural, foster and adoptive families. Family placement is concerned with more than home finding for children; it is concerned with promoting the development and easing the pain of all family members of first and new families.

Some reflections

If this last statement is true, it is pertinent to ask what differences have resulted from the amalgamation of the personal social services and the thinking behind the Children Act, 1975. Any judgement can only be a subjective response to the material received.

The impression gained was that fostering and adoption were being conceived of as a broadly based service of intervention in family situations rather than a narrowly based homefinding exercise for children. A network of inter-relationships was developing rather than a highly controlled child exchange arrangement. It seemed to be becoming less easy to separate out the needs of one individual and organize services around those needs when, at least potentially, everyone involved was a possible client of the personal social services departments. People are not only possible clients but also possible resources for help. Family placement seems to be an area where opportunities for reciprocal service can be developed.

Secondly, the beginnings of a strategy may be perceptible but a strategy with so many variants and degrees of emphasis that no pattern could be regarded as even near universal at this stage. With this reservation, there did appear to be a move towards using fostering for a specified time and for a specified purpose and within a framework of services. This framework of services may be summarised as:

1. the use of neighbourhood, domiciliary and day care resources to support families and children in their own homes;

2. the development of local fostering as a community resource to offer short-term alternative care and treatment within a family setting;

3. time limited fostering as a method of treatment to achieve agreed goals including preparation for another stage;

4. the continued use of indeterminate fostering but with increased questioning of the need for permanence.

Such a strategy outlined in this way makes light of the constant decision making required and suggests a series of sequential stages. Rather, it is intended to suggest a set of options regarded as complementary to each other and to be balanced against alternatives in residential care or within the health or education services. A strategy of this kind, while it may provide a useful practical guide, has draw-backs. It omits the option of adoption which still seems to be an outside choice and not yet fully integrated into professional thinking and practice. In an integrated family placement approach, adoption could be one of the alternatives to be considered instead of domiciliary or day care if, in a particular case, the interests of the child and his family are considered in a long term context over and above a sequential set of remedies used to defer decision making until drift rather than constructive planning has taken over. This kind of long term planning is full of pain. Although this is purely speculative, it may be that one of the defences against pain and anxiety is the continued separation, both in organization and thinking, of fostering, adoption and residential care. One of the functions of specialized fostering and adoption officers and special units may be to work at the management of interdependent rather than polarized resources for families and children.

What is the effect of contact between all parties to family placement and social service departments? The inquiry provided few answers as far as natural parents and local communities, schools and other services were concerned. From the evidence quoted, foster parents and adoptive parents acknowledged satisfactions and a number of frustrations; children have only recently become vocal but research has long shown that they have suffered from too many moves. For family placement to survive and develop in large bureaucratic organizations and in small and sometimes rigid agencies, it has to be managed with a high degree of consultation and shared decision making if it is to avoid alienation through the fear of forfeit of rights or exercise of choice. These are often dimensions beyond traditional skills associated with fostering and adoption. Perhaps the simplest way of raising this question is to ask whether agencies can manage family placement in such a way that all those whose lives are affected feel they have had some recognition and help with their feelings of loss and have gained some experience of value and worthy of respect. There is a particularly crucial testing time at the age of eighteen or nineteen years. Are the personal social services seen as available to offer help throughout life or does the individual suddenly become a new client of, for example, the mental health section which seems unrelated to past experiences?

Finally, in terms of future policy development, there is the prospect of developing family care for other client groups. Such a prospect could be attractive in itself and also opportune at a time when unemployment may give a boost to home based occupations. Family placement for children, in the past, has suffered too much from lack of model building, research and evaluation. Is it too much to hope that this situation is now changing with regard to the placement of children and that the practice of developing a model, describing the processes and methods of testing the results could become a basis for developments in family care and treatment for children and adults?

Many of the issues raised in this report emerge within the specific context of the new developments and initiatives described. However, there are several much more basic issues concerning patterns of family placement which have a wider historical perspective: the relationship of fostering and adoption to each other; the appropriateness of each to the developmental needs of individual children; the role of family placement within the whole range of services available to children in care and their families; the quality of care and treatment in family placement however diversified the patterns may become; the unavoidable conflicts of interest in trying to meet the rights of all those involved; in view of these conflicts, the need for hard decision-making at an early enough stage in order to avoid drift and damage; the rewards due to placement families; the demands of time, money and skill that investment in a family placement policy demands of agencies.

Perhaps in the long term the most important of all is the development of practice to enable family placement to warrant public approval and to provide individual fulfillment.

References

Adamson, G. (1973). *The Care-Takers: A study of the Sociological and Psychological Aspects of Foster Home Care, and its Organisation within Children's Departments and Social Services Departments.* London: Bookstall Publications.

Association of British Adoption and Fostering Agencies (1977). *Fostering in the 70s and Beyond: A Descriptive Analysis of the Current Scene.* London.

Association of British Adoption and Fostering Agencies (1977). *The Soul Kids Campaign.*

Bohman, M. (1970). *Adopted Children and their Families: A Follow-up Study of Adopted Children, their Background, Environment, and Adjustment.* Stockholm: Propius.

Children in Care in England and Wales (March 1976). London: HMSO.

Community Relations Commission (1975). *Fostering Black Children.* London.

Department of Health and Social Security, Scottish Education Department (Social Work Services Group), Welsh Office: Working Party on Fostering Practice (1976). *Foster Care: A Guide to Practice.* London. HMSO.

Department of Health and Social Security (1976). *Access to Birth Records: Notes for Counsellors.* London: Department of Health and Social Security.

Donley, K. (1975). *Opening New Doors: Finding Families for Older and Handicapped Children.* London: The Association of British Adoption and Fostering Agencies.

Fanshel, D. and Shinn, E. B. (1978). *Children in Foster Care: A Longitudinal Investigation.* New York: Columbia University Press.

George, V. (1970). *Foster Care: Theory and Practice.* London: Routledge and Kegan Paul.

Hazel, N. (1975) 'Into Europe. Residential care as the key to fostering: the German experience', *Social Work Today,* 5, 25, 771–772.

Hazel, N. and Cox, R. (1976). *The Special Family Placement Project: Progress Report for 1975.* Maidstone: Kent Social Services Department.

Hazel, N., Cox, R. and Ashley-Mudie, P. (1977). *Second Report of the Special Family Project*. Maidstone: Kent Social Services Department.

Holman, R. (1973). *Trading in Children*. London: Routledge and Kegan Paul.

Holman, R. (1975). 'The place of fostering in social work', *British Journal of Social Work,* 5, 1, 3–29.

Home Office and Scottish Education Department (1972). *Report of the Departmental Committee on the Adoption of Children*. (Houghton Report). London: HMSO.

Jaffee, B. and Fanshel, D. (1970). *How they Fared in Adoption: A Follow-up Study*. New York: Columbia University Press.

Kadushin, A. (1970). *Adopting Older Children*. New York: Columbia University Press.

Kalveston, A-L. (1976). *Caring for Children with Special Needs: A Study of 40 Swedish Foster Families*. Brussels, Institut Europeen Interuniversitaire de l'Action Sociale.

Kraus, J. (1971). 'Predicting success of foster placements for school age children', *Social Work,* 16, 1, 63–72.

Morrison, M. S. (1978). *Stretching the Limits*. Edinburgh. South East Scotland Resource Centre.

Napier, H. (1972). 'Success and failure in foster care', *British Journal of Social Work,* 2, 2, 187–204.

National Foster Care Association (1977). *Education and Training in Foster Care: A Report with Recommendations*. London: National Foster Care Association.

Newman, N. and Mackintosh, H. (1975). *A Roof Over Their Heads? Residential Provision for Children in S.E. Scotland*. Edinburgh: University of Edinburgh, Dept. of Social Administration.

Page, R. and Clark, G. A. (eds.) (1977). *Who Cares? Young People in Care Speak Out*. London: National Children's Bureau.

Portsmouth Polytechnic and Portsmouth Department of Social Studies (1973). *Portsmouth Fostering Study*. Portsmouth.

Pringle, M. L. Kellmer. (1974). *The Needs of Children*. London: Hutchinson.

Prosser, H. (1978). *Perspectives on Foster Care: An Annotated Bibliography*. Windsor. NFER Pub. Co. Ltd.

Pugh, G. (1977). 'Professional fostering-defining objectives', *Adoption and Fostering,* 88, 18–20.

Rapoport, R. and R. N., Strelitz, A. (1977). *Fathers, Mothers and Others: Towards New Alliances*. London: Routledge and Kegan Paul.

Reid, W. J. and Epstein, L. (1972). *Task-Centred Casework*. London and New York: Columbia University Press.

Rowe, J. and Lambert, L. (1973). *Children Who Wait: A Study of Children Needing Substitute Families*. London: Association of British Adoption Agencies.

Rutter, M. (1972). *Maternal Deprivation Re-assessed*. London: Penguin.

Seed, P. and Thomson, M. (1977). *All Kinds of Care*. Aberdeen: University of Aberdeen, Dept. of Social Work.

Seglow, J., Pringle, M. L. Kellmer and Wedge, P. (1972). *Growing Up Adopted: A Long-term National Study of Adopted Children and their Families*. Windsor, NFER Pub. Co. Ltd.

Shapiro, D. (1976). *Agencies and Foster Children*. New York: Columbia University Press.

Smith, C. R. (1976). 'Adoption advice: a new service', *The British Journal of Social Work*, 6, 2, 157–175.

Specht, H. and Vickery, A. (eds.) (1977). *Integrating Social Work Methods*. London: Allen and Unwin.

Tizard, B. (1977) *Adoption: A Second Chance*. London: Open Books.

Triseliotis, J. P. (1970). *Evaluation of Adoption Policy and Practice*. Edinburgh: University of Edinburgh, Dept. of Social Administration.

Appendices

1. Tables

2. The Written Inquiry

3. Useful addresses

Appendix 1
Tables

Table 1

Children adopted in England and Wales, 1959–1977

Year	Total Children	Legitimate Children* Joint adopters		Illegitimate Children* Joint adopters	
		One or both a parent	Neither a parent	One or both a parent	Neither a parent
1959	14,109	1,541	1,289	3,105	7,887
1960	15,099	1,576	1,517	2,787	8,990
1961	16,000	1,545	1,420	2,799	9,980
1962	16,894	1,585	1,447	2,674	10,984
1963	17,782	1,888	1,438	2,636	11,569
1964	20,412	2,291	1,569	2,951	13,408
1965	21,032	2,552	1,574	3,173	13,537
1966	22,792	3,097	1,750	3,679	14,034
1967	22,802	3,090	1,355	3,963	14,144
1968	24,831	4,038	1,390	4,479	14,641
1969	23,708	4,558	1,207	4,649	13,047
1970	22,373	5,202	1,179	5,054	10,711
1971	21,495	5,481	1,074	5,204	9,573
1972	21,599	6,792	1,097	5,441	8,114
1973	22,247	8,101	1,118	5,576	7,341
1974	22,502	9,114	887	5,691	6,621
1975	21,299	9,262	806	5,305	5,774
1976	17,621	7,838	884	3,989	4,777
1977	12,748	4,545	841	3,238	4,026

* Joint adopters only.
Sources: The Registrar General's *Statistical Review of England and Wales* for the years *1959 to 1973*; OPCS Monitors FM3.

Number of adoption orders made by Scottish courts, 1966 and 1976.

Year	Total
1966	2,040
1976	1,612

Source: Scottish Office, Social Work Services Group.

Table 2
Illegitimate births and illegitimate children adopted by non-parents.
England and Wales, 1967–1977.

Year	Illegitimate births	Illegitimate children adopted by non-parents
1967	69,928	14,222
1968	69,806	14,751
1969	67,041	13,129
1970	64,744	10,797
1971	65,678	9,642
1972	62,511	8,170
1973	58,100	7,388
1974	56,500	6,621*
1975	54,891	5,774*
1976	53,800	4,777*
1977		4,026

* Joint adoptions only.

Sources: The Registrar General's *Statistical Review of England and Wales,* for the years *1958* to *1973*: OPCS Monitors FM3; Population Trends No 2, HMSO 1976.

Table 3
Comparative statistics of children received into care in England and Wales: as at 31 March 1956, 1966 and 1976.

	1956	1966	1976
1. Proportion of all children received into local authority care during the preceding year who were under the age of 5 years	55% (21,200)	55% (30,000)	36% (18,800)
2. Proportion of children in local authority care at 31st March who were under the age of 5 years	18% (11,200)	22% (15,300)	12% (12,400)
3. Proportion of children received into local authority care in the preceding year who were over school leaving age*	2% (900)	4% (2,100)	4% (2,300)
4. Proportion of children in local authority care at 31st March who were over school leaving age	20% (12,500)	21% (14,600)	20% (20,200)
5. Proportion of boys among children in local authority care at 31st March	55% (34,600)	55% (38,000)	61% (61,000)
6. Proportion of all children admitted to local authority care in the preceding year who were committed by the courts	8% (3,100)	9% (4,700)	25% (12,900)
7. Proportion of all children in care at 31st March who were committed by the courts	30% (18,700)	32% (22,400)	51% (51,600)
8. Proportion of all children admitted to care during the preceding year who were committed by the courts as offenders	n/a	3% (1,400)	11% (5,600)
9. Proportion of all children admitted to care during the preceding year who were committed by the courts under care proceedings.	n/a	6% (3,300)	14% (7,200)

	1956	1966	1976
10. Proportion of all committed children in care at 31st March who were allowed to be in the care of a parent, relative or friend	n/a	20% (4,400)	35% (18,000)
11. Proportion of all children in care on 31st March who were boarded-out	43% (27,100)	46% (31,800)	33% (33,100)
12. Proportion of all children in care on 31st March who were boarded-out with a relative	9% (5,800)	7% (5,100)	4% (4,400)
13. Proportion of all children in care on 31st March who were actually living with a parent, guardian, relative or friend.	n/a	14% (9,500)	22% (22,300)
14. Proportion of all children in care on 31st March who were accommodated in residential homes*	46% (28,500)	39% (27,000)	41% (40,900)
15. Children accommodated in residential nurseries on 31st March as a proportion of all children in care under 5 years	40% (4,400)	20% (3,000)	15% (1,900)
16. Proportion of children discharged during the preceding year who had reached the ages of 18 or 19.	10% (3,800)	8% (4,300)	16% (8,300)

Source: compiled from *Children in Care of Local Authorities in England and Wales: 1956* Cmnd. 9881, *1966,* Cmnd, 3204; *1976* H.C. 506 by Professor Roy Parker, for the National Children's Bureau.

Note: * The school leaving age was raised from 15 to 16 as from the start of the new academic year 1972. Thus 1973 was the first full year of the new requirements. Before then it was plain that children received into care over school leaving age meant the 15, 16 and 17 year olds. The statistics for the year ending 31st March 1973 continued with the same designation so that one might assume that half of that year's intake were only the 16 and 17 year olds. One would expect to see a reduction in the numbers. In 1974 the statistics noted for the first time the age groups of children coming into care in the preceding year as at 31st March 1974. This will mean that some 15-year-olds are still included. The variation in specifying ages at reception since 1974 may have the general effect of slightly exaggerating the number of older children coming into care (Items 1 and 3).

Table 4:
Children in care in Scotland in 1966 and 1976.

	Children in care or under supervision	Children 'boarded out' or in 'foster care'*	Percentage 'fostered' or 'boarded out'*
1966	10,654	6,385	60
1976 (provisional)	16,983	3,660	22

* 1966 figures are of children 'boarded out' etc. with relatives or other persons; 1976 figures are of children 'in foster care'.

Source: Scottish Office, Social Work Services Group. *NB*: Between 1966 and 1976 there were important changes in the measuring system and in definitions used; appropriate care is therefore needed in interpreting this table.

Table 5
Children in the care of the local authorities in England and Wales on 31 March 1970–1976.

Year	Total	Under 2 years	Aged 2 but not of compulsory school age	Of compulsory school age	Over compulsory school age	Percentage boarded out*
1970	71,210	4,555	9,105	43,175	14,375	48
1971	87,377	4,377	8,951	49,968	24,081	41
1972	90,586	3,837	8,320	51,858	26,571	41
1973	93,188	3,960	8,635	59,325	21,268	40
1974	95,867	3,900	7,830	63,620	20,517	40
1975	99,120	4,030	8,280	66,947	19,863	40
1976	100,628	4,030	8,353	68,060	20,185	41

* Rounded off percentages.

(From *Children in Care in England and Wales*. Annual Reports HMSO).
The latest available comparative costs of boarding out and residential costs (*Children in Care in England and Wales*, March 1976) quote £8.80 as the average cost of a boarded out child (1975–76) excluding administrative, fieldwork and miscellaneous items (pocket money, holiday); and the cost per child week in residential accommodation as £65.00 weekly.

Table 6
Statistical details of adoption placements made by the Church of England Children's Society 1967-1977.

	1967	1968	1969	1970	1971	1972	1973	1974	1975	1976	1977	Totals
Ordinary adoptions	524	444	297	285	244	230	211	277	193	198	199	3,102
Children with special needs*	182	192	160	201	239	231	168	149	95	109	85	1,811
Combined totals	706	636	457	486	483	461	379	426	288	307	284	4,913
(a)	(29)	(32)	(42)	(53)	(61)	(73)	(58)	(51)	(44)	(51)	(39)	

Included within the figures for children with special needs are 494 mixed race children and the yearly placements of those children are recorded under (a).

* Children with special needs:
   1. Child in the five plus age range.
   2. Child with specific ailment, either mental or physical.
   3. Child of mixed race or fully coloured.
   4. Doubts concerning development.
   5. Perinatal difficulties.

Source: Church of England Children's Society.

Table 7

Results of Granada 'World in Action' Programmes

(As known to ARE on 31 March, 1976.)

1.	**First Programme (May 1974)**	

Applications sent to member agencies: 1559

Approved for adoption		124
Approved for fostering		71
	Total:	195
Children placed for adoption		70
Children placed for fostering		59
	Total:	129

2.	**Second Programme (February 1975)**	

Applications sent to member agencies: 308

Approved for adoption		48
Approved for fostering		6
	Total:	54
Children placed for adoption		10
Children placed for fostering		6
	Total:	16

Source: Adoption Resource Exchange.

Appendix 2
National Children's Bureau
Inquiry into current issues in fostering and adoption

We would be grateful if you could supply us with the following information:

1. Do you have any handbooks or committee reports which outline your current policies on placing children for fostering or adoption? If so, may we see copies? These will be used in confidence and authorities and societies will not be quoted by name in our report.

2. (a) What officers or groups within your department are charged with responsibility for development of policy and practice in the fields of fostering and adoption? (b) What is the role, function and level within the department of any specialist fostering and adoption staff? (c) Whom would we contact, should we wish to follow-up your reply? Please give name, position, address and phone number.

*3. Can you give us details of: (a) any developments in procedure or practice in the last few years in the field of fostering and adoption, either at headquarters or in area teams; (b) any new schemes that you are currently considering; (c) any innovations that you would like to set in hand if resources were available.

*4. (a) Is any research or inquiry currently being undertaken within your authority or society in the field of fostering or adoption, either by your own staff or by others, e.g. a university or polytechnic? If so please give details. (b) Has any such research been completed within the last five years and has it been published? If so please give details. (c) Is there any such research that you would like to see undertaken?

Developments on which you have details might include some of the following:

Systematic identification of children in the care of your authority who would benefit from adoption or fostering.

Planning the placements of all children in care, both within the authority and in co-operation with neighbouring authorities and voluntary organizations.

Recruitment of foster or adoptive parents, including publicity campaign.

Selection and assessment of foster or adoptive parents.

Training of and support for foster or adoptive parents, including support after adoptive placements.

The use of group work with foster or adoptive parents, both for selection and support.

Consultation with foster and adoptive parents with regard to planning policy.

Involvement of foster or adoptive parents in decision making and planning.

Consultation with children about their placements.

Finding homes for 'children with special needs' — disturbed and distruptive children, older children, sibling groups, handicapped children, children from minority groups.

Professional or salaried foster parent schemes.

Use of foster placements for assessment purposes.

Training of specialist and support staff.

Review arrangements for placements.

Formalised arrangements with voluntary societies.

Any innovations resulting from the 1975 Children Act.

Appendix 3
List of useful addresses

Adoption Resource Exchange, 40 Brunswick Square, London WC1N 1AZ
Telephone: 01-839-0496

Association of British Adoption & Fostering Agencies, 4 Southampton
Row, London WC1B 4AA
Telephone: 01-242-8951

Commission for Racial Equality, Elliot House, 10/12 Allington Street,
London SW1E 5EH
Telephone: 01-828-7022

Clearing House for Local Authorities, Social Services Research, University
of Birmingham, P.O. Box 363, Birmingham B15 2TT
Telephone: 021-472-1301

National Foster Care Association, 129 Queen's Crescent, London NW5
4HE
Telephone: 01-485-3929

Parents for Children, 222 Camden High Street, London NW1 8QR
Telephone: 011-485-7526

Parent to Parent Information on Adoption Services, 26 Belsize Grove,
London NW3 4TR
Telephone: 01-722-5328

South East Scotland Resource Centre, 21 Castle Street, Edinburgh EH2
3DN
Telephone: 031-225-6441